West Brom's
Greatest Games

West Brom's Greatest Games

Foreword by Willie Johnston

Simon Wright

Know The Score Books Limited
118 Alcester Road
Studley, Warwickshire B80 7NT
01527 454482
info@knowthescorebooks.com
www.knowthescorebooks.com

A CIP catalogue record is available for this book from the British Library
ISBN: 978-1-84818-206-6

Printed and bound in Great Britain
Athenaeum Press, Gateshead, Tyne & Wear

CONTENTS

FOREWORD

AYE, WEST Bromwich Albion … I had the best footballing days of my life there. Better than Rangers, better than Hearts … even better than Vancouver. Yet I'm a heady Scot who's played for some of the biggest clubs north of the Border, with the caps and medals to show for it.

Simply, England is a bigger stage to play on, with bigger clubs … and, OK – bigger wages, too. You get noticed in England. Not that I had much choice about moving there. I was literally a marked man in the Scottish League, and my next grumble about my rough treatment would probably have meant the return of capital punishment.

It was hard for me at first. There was relegation. Rangers don't do relegation, and it's not an experience I recommend. Everyone was miserable for months on end and I ended up making my own kids miserable too. And Don Howe was in charge (Don Howe … I tell you my next book is going to be called: *Why I Didn't Like Don Howe* … starting with my suggestion that if you're going to sign someone, it's a good idea to watch them first). As well as that, my new rented house was in a decent area, good neighbours, but the previous owner had painted the entire house black and gold. Matched his car the neighbours reckoned. That was downright odd, even in the colourful 1970s. The house owner was Bobby Gould, and the other lads reckoned he was always like that. Gouldy didn't stick around long after I'd arrived – he sold me the house, and got out of town, not leaving me so much as a paint brush or any turps.

When Don Howe also got out of town, fortunes changed for both club and me. Once Johnny Giles got myself and the club moving forward, I was enjoying my game again, and I was enjoying life. Football is about entertainment, not systems or blackboards, and Johnny didn't try to change me on the field or off it... And, aye... OK, he could drink me under the table, as well. I was never much of a drinker. I had so much respect for the guy that when he asked me to do a marking job on an opposition player, I just got on with it. I mean – me, doing a marking job? Only for you, wee man. By now, I'd been around Sassenachs long enough to actually understand what they were saying and even referees weren't quite as regular a pain in the arse as they were in Scotland. Save time guys and get my name in your book in the dressing room before kick-off, why dontcha?

Of course, West Bromwich Albion got back into the top Division by winning at Oldham, and that was naturally the first match in the book I turned to. What a day, and what a party afterwards. Let me say, here and now, there was no way I would have been sent off that day despite what it says in this book. I was on such a high that I could have been kicked all day and all night and I wouldn't have noticed. I didn't really need a beer that night but had one anyway. No problem with beer on the bus in those days and all the way back on the motorway it was like the biggest mobile bar in the world.

After Oldham, I had a read of the muddy game against Manchester United in the Cup. I remember finding bits of mud still on me days after the game. Beating United was no big deal, then – *only* Man United, and Albion are their bogey team. I don't know where the author dragged up this quote from me after the first match at Old Trafford, saying we'd beat them in the replay, but it still makes perfect sense to me even now. I leave stats to other people, but it seemed like when I was around, every time it was Albion against United, home or away, it was the Reds who needed to be worried. We knocked them out of the FA Cup in the mud and famously beat them 5-3 on their own pitch, and you can reminisce more about both games inside this book. On top of that, we gubbed them 4-0 at home two years in a row. We were just too good for them. In the 1977/78 season (I got someone to look this up for me), we drew twice in Manchester, and beat them twice at the Hawthorns. Can't repeat what United's Scottish lads were saying to me after we beat 'em yet again. It just isn't right for a book like this.

Bogeys, and Scotland... that reminds me. People tell me there are proper decent golf courses in the Midlands now, but when I was living in Dunchurch Road, Sutton Coldfield, there was nothing. That comes hard when you're used to taking on the best courses in the world whenever you feel like it. Count your blessings gentlemen, and try to appreciate what you've got now.

Although I've been back among my own kith and kin for decades now, West Bromwich Albion has never really left me. You supporters certainly haven't. It's so good to see so many of you visiting the Port Brae – and there's always room for more of ye! Normally, in the Kingdom of Fife, we don't take kindly to ootrels (that's 'strangers' to you), but there's always a welcome in my pub for people from the Black Country.

Finally, I know first-hand how much time and work goes into putting a book together (have you all bought *Sent Off At Gunpoint* yet?), so I can only wish Simon Wright all the best with this one. Meant a lot to me, looking back on all the great games, catching up again on the details that I'd forgotten, and I'm sure you will do the same.

Here's tae ye, Albion fans.

Willie Johnston

INTRODUCTION

GREATEST MATCHES. When my publisher first floated the idea to me, I was a little dubious. Greatest? Even the word's not 'great' any more, easy enough to chuck around, yet beset with a multiplicity of meanings, rather like 'green' or 'digital'. A word cheapened by instinctive links to trash TV – '50 Greatest Films', '50 Best Dustbin Lids', '50 Worst Soap Operas', anyone? Just as I needed to better define 'Cult Hero' for my first book, so I required an improved definition to kick off my match selection process. In the end after much pondering, I plumped for 'Richly Enjoyable'. While the great British public is unlikely to instinctively rummage in their pockets for cash to snap up copies of *West Bromwich Albion's 50 Richly Enjoyable Games*, sticking to my definition aided the winnowing-down process enormously. Well, a teensy bit. There's an awful lot to choose from.

It's only when you take a high-powered microscope to the Baggies' history that you truly get to appreciate the magnificent heritage of this extraordinary Black Country institution, and understand just how many eventful matches there are to choose from. To the eternal credit of my publisher, he was keen to feature snapshots across the entire 130-year club history, not just the easy, populist, post war period stuff. So that's precisely what I've done.

The trophy, or promotion winning matches, picked themselves. Beyond that, richly enjoyable football doesn't include any defeats, not in my book. Literally. Mind you, I did make one exception to that rule: going out of the play-offs at the Reebok didn't feel like a defeat at the time to those who were there, and sung like Cup Winners. As the optimists claimed that night, this was just the end of the beginning … and they were quite correct. Of course, beyond the obvious, my selection is subjective, so no apologies from me if your particular favourite isn't included here. My own original shortlist ran to almost 100 matches. It's not easy at all to squeeze down to so few; a bit like deciding who gets the kidney machine, if you like.

Apropos our Championship-winning season, I felt sufficiently justified to include 14 different fixtures, all of which were all richly enjoyable in their own way, but a severe outbreak of pragmatism finally forced me to settle for just three. Given my well-known penchant for smaller clubs, I would have liked to include the 3-2 at Scunthorpe as a richly enjoyable battle played within a small enclosed ground. Likewise, the 5-1 demolition of the same claret and blue mob in the return fixture was a superb example of just how richly flamboyant and exciting a Mowbray team really can be. My interest in clubs and quirky fixtures that don't always make the head-lines is reflected elsewhere in the book, with the inclusion of the Plymouth FA Cup match (supporters at their most determined and passionate being well rewarded for determination to just be there), and Brescia in the Anglo-Italian. The latter had an attendance of only 160, yet stood out for a whole host of reasons, not least of which was a unique feeling of complete oneness with the team, and an absolute gift from the gods: the opportunity to annoy Stoke City – always to be commended.

Although some Michelin Star-obsessed food critics would have you believe differently, it's still perfectly possible to derive precisely the same amount of gustatory pleasure from a well cooked plate of fish and chips as anything expensively thrown together by Gordon Ramsay et al. In much the same way, a big crowd and a Premier League stage aren't essential accompaniments to a genuinely entertaining game, a view that's very contrary to modern belief, sadly. Only one match out of 150+ spread over four largely frustrating seasons of Premier League football makes the cut, which speaks volumes, I suppose. I would have liked to take the off-beat project a stage further, but lacked sufficient nerve to include a reserve game or even an FA Youth Cup match. When 'quirky' includes a young player (who later became an England international) actually soiling his shorts on the pitch I was seriously tempted.

Such a book can never be a solo project, so grateful thanks for the various observations of my erudite sounding-boards, better-known as Steve Carr, Colin Mackenzie, Dave Watkins, Terry Wills and Neil

Reynolds. Collectively, they have first hand experience of around 10,000 games. In addition, Terry gave me unfettered access to his magnificent 1960s scrapbooks. Such is the enormity of his collection, rumour has it that El Tel is the sole person in these parts with a loft extending into hyperspace. Steve and Colin were again to the fore in supplying vast quantities of mainly unpublished match information, teams and referees, although it should be said that the third category regularly defeated even the combined mental outpourings of those august statisticians. Steve (bravely, just before he became a married man!) handled the factual proofreading, while Katrina Baker courageously volunteered to check my grammar.

The infamous Alan Buckley phrase, 'you know nothing about football' describes Katrina perfectly, but she knows her hyphens, so defiantly hung-in-there amidst 50,000 words-absolutely dripping-with football-references. Somehow we're still good mates. There's only one person to go to for Albion photographs, so take a bow Laurie Rampling. Heaven knows from where he obtains some of his illustrations; perhaps 'heaven' being the operative word! It's just a shame there wasn't room to use more. To his credit, publisher Simon Lowe basically left the words to me. He didn't even protest about regular Michael-extracting mentions of his team. Must also thank the 'Boss' as in Glynis Wright, for intelligently listening to my wails during days of writer's block.

The support from so many supporters is all important. In an age where the loyalties of players, managers – club owners, even – are as ephemeral as a politician's promise, changing in the twinkling of an eye, fans are the only consistent part of modern football. We are Albion. And if you're a real Albionite, I'm convinced you'll enjoy my summary of the best bits of the Baggies. Or if you prefer... *The Greatest Bits.*

Simon Wright

v Stoke 3-2

Staffordshire Cup Final. Att: 6,150
April 21 1883

Albion	Stoke	Referee
Roberts	Wildin	W. Pierce Dix (who later
Harry Bell	Stanford	joined the Albion
Stanton	Mellor	Secretarial staff)
E. Horton	Brown	
Bunn	Bettany	
While	Johnson	
Aston	Brown	
Whitehouse	Shutt	
Timmins	Fennall	
Bisseker	Myatt	
George Bell	Bennett	

IN THE absence of the Football League and the FA Cup (which the club had yet to enter) the biggest trophies around for a Staffordshire-based football club were the Birmingham Cup and Staffordshire Cup. Albion had been defeated in the quarter-final of the Birmingham Cup but in the Staffs Cup, they'd reached their first ever Cup final.

For an embryonic club like West Bromwich Albion to be so close to winning the trophy – their first ever – served as both reward and justification for their founders. Big name clubs like Stoke City (twice) Aston Villa and the then well known Wednesbury Old Athletic had all previously lifted this trophy. To reach the final in Stoke, the stars in red and white hoops had played six ties including the first ever meetings with Cup favourites Aston Villa (a 3-3 draw followed by a famous 1-0 victory at Albion's own Four Acres ground).

The *Midland Athletic Star* was convinced that 'the clever West Bromwich men would win rather easily.' Albion's directors wanted their first trophy so badly that the players were despatched to Malvern for a week's special training. In an age of amateur players receiving pennies for expenses only, this was an enormous investment. But there was more. Two first class rail compartments were reserved for the team (though the club members were only offered third class accommodation).

West Bromwich approached the London and North West railway who were delighted to provide special trains picking up at both Spon Lane (West Bromwich) and Oldbury. Standard fare was the equivalent of 13p but with an executive option at 25p for those who wished to travel with the team in the first class salons. Buoyed by an advertisement in the *West Bromwich Free Press*, Albion supporters were quick to take up the offer to get to the big match. The *Midland Athletic Star* estimated between 1,500 and 2,000 people travelled from the Black Country, a remarkable turnout during an era when most Black Country people rarely if ever left their town of birth. It was unfortunate that after all their preparation and investment by the directors nobody had considered how the players would get to the Victoria Ground from the station…

Over 6,000 people assembled for the big Cup final, including 500 who had taken advantage of a special train from Leek. The Moorlands town was then a hotbed of football with three teams competing in the Staffs Cup. Two of their teams had been defeated in the semi-final.

Albion won the toss and decided to defend the town end. Their enormous goalkeeper Bob Roberts was quickly under pressure. The future England international made numerous fine stops (including one concerted spell of five saves in two minutes) before eventually being beaten by JOHNSON.

Fortunately, TIMMINS of West Bromwich quickly put the visitors level. Just three minutes later, Black Country caps were airborne as Horton's left wing corner set up BUNN perfectly to put West Bromwich ahead. Back came Stoke again with JOHNSON levelling. 'A faster and more exciting game has rarely been seen on the Stoke ground', observed the *Midland Athletic Star*, a statement which still rings true over a century later.

Albion's George Bell had a goal disallowed for offside as the end to end play continued. There were only 15 minutes remaining when BELL notched the winner for the youthful Black Country club. Accounts vary about this Cup-winning goal but the most graphic reads: 'a long straight shot by Aston with George Bell racing in to head through the goal amid the deafening cheers of the Black Country people.' Despite the Potters' best efforts, Roberts and co kept them comfortably at bay for the rest of the match. Indeed, following a Stoke corner, Albion counter-attacked cleverly. Aston charged down the right wing and crossed to his team-mate

Bisseker … who was unfortunately swamped by excited spectators running onto the pitch before he could shoot.

Fortunately, this early incident of hooliganism didn't alter the outcome of the Cup final. Albion were about to lift their first ever trophy. Alderman Minton presented the Staffordshire Cup to captain John While and the players were carried off the pitch by triumphant supporters.

Such a feat deserved a celebration and the Albion Cup Winners retired to the Copeland Arms in Stoke where they were invited to drink from the champagne-filled trophy. History doesn't record the emotions of the club's founding fathers at this point although it's easy to imagine that cup being refilled as quickly as it was emptied. What is recorded is that the players were singularly unimpressed with the quality of the medals. The Board agreed to press the Staffs FA later for mementoes which would more properly mark the occasion.

There were more celebrations to follow. The possibly tired and emotional players returned to Spon Lane at half past ten that night. Waiting for them was a sponsored brake (stagecoach) pulled by four grey horses. Also waiting were thousands of supporters who lined either side of Spon Lane and West Bromwich High Street. They cheered wildly as their winning team passed them by. Coloured lights beamed from many windows along the route. The Dartmouth Park band preceded the triumphant team, playing *See the Conquering Hero Come.* New boys West Bromwich Albion were now an intrinsic part of town pride.

The club's first trophy was ample reason for the first ever club photograph, which was taken later in front of Mr Samuel Keys's residence, Highfield House (Keys was the father of Harry Keys, later to become Albion Chairman). At least two different photographs were taken. Each of the players was presented with a cabinet photo of the cup-winning team at the club's annual dinner in June. The President of the Wednesbury Charity Association, Isaac Griffiths, declared during the AGM that Albion "appeared almost comet-like on the football world but, unlike a comet, it had not suddenly disappeared."

v Preston North End 2-1

FA Cup Final. Att: 19,000
24 March 1888

Albion	Preston North End	Referee
Roberts	Dr Mills-Roberts	Major Marindin
Aldridge	Howarth	
Green	N. Ross	
Horton	Holmes	
Perry	Russell	
Timmins	Graham	
Woodhall	Gordon	
Bassett	J. Ross	
Bayliss	Goodall	
Pearson	Dewhurst	
Wilson	Drummond	

FROM THE *Athletic News*, 20 March 1988: 'Of course, everybody is backing North End, and, on form, it is quite 2 to 1 on, but my advice is, don't back a favourite for the English Final unless it is at evens. There is a great luck in football, and non-favourites have won every year for the last six years. Besides, West Bromwich Albion are not defeated until the 90 minutes have expired.'

These even-handed words were a rare tonic, a glorious exception from the plethora of pro-Preston pronouncements. That this was Albion's third consecutive FA Cup final was considered secondary to the dominant power of North End – 'The Invincibles'. With their imported Scottish players, the Lancastrians were unbeaten in their previous 40 matches. PNE won 38 of those 40 matches and scored over 200 goals – an average of 5 goals per match.

These were embryonic days for professional football. The Black Country lads (average height 5 foot 9 inches, average weight 12 stone) earned the equivalent of 50p a week for their football activities in addition to their regular job, so the dangled Cup Winners' bonus, equivalent to five weeks' pay was highly desirable. Star teenager Billy Bassett was only 5 foot 6 inches tall, weighing 10 stone. Only one man, Ezra Horton, was older than 25 (though admittedly life expectancy during this decade was only 40). Every man was born within four miles of Albion's ground with half of them attending the same West Bromwich school. This was a genuine local team.

Then, as now, the club was careful with their income. JJ Bentley, President of the Football League observed their arrival at Euston Square: "We saw a small band of boys emerge from the platform, each carrying an insignificant bag. When we were informed that these boys, acting as their own porters, were our opponents at the Oval, our confidence increased. They had a simple two-horse waggonette at the Oval, Preston had a prancing four-in-hand."

Sport and Play observed the Cup final scene at the Oval: 'It was a rare sight – the level green meadow, the immense masses of people piled tier upon tier till they reached the very edge of the huge enclosure, the excited buzz of the assembled thousands, the hundreds of newspapers flashing white in the strong light like the crest of billows in that great sea of humanity, and the afternoon sun shining down warm and radiant on it all.' There was singing too – the most popular being the bawdy music hall ditty, *Two Lovely Black Eyes.*

Such was the size of the crowd for the 3.30pm kick-off that the gates were closed, the first recorded instance of this occurrence in England for a football match. Some 19,000 were present including three workmen from the Black Country, who, unable to afford rail travel, walked from West Bromwich. The Baggies lost the toss and thus spent the first half attacking uphill, facing a slight wind and bright sunshine. Despite these irritations, the Black Country men took the lead in the 17th minute. Teenager Bassett beat his opponent Graham and centred perfectly for JEM BAYLISS to fire past the Preston keeper Mills-Roberts.

Preston hit back but found the huge frame of Albion goalkeeper Bob Roberts a hard barrier to overcome. Frustrated, they lost both their poise and their heads. *Sport and Play* noted: 'The play of the North End players was nothing short of brutal and Graham in particular. Once he came at Woodhall with clenched teeth and a look of fierceness. I positively shuddered. I saw [referee] Major Marindin giving some of them a bit of his mind on occasions.' Referees were seen not heard in this period so any intervention was considered thoroughly bad form.

Cooling words during the interval gave the 'Invincibles' new spirit and they attacked the Baggies with fresh gusto. They finally found an equaliser after a Preston forward charged into and felled Bob Roberts and GOODALL pounced to score. Major Mandarin waved away all appeals.

Sensing victory, the Lancastrians poured into the attack. Albion were hard pressed, notably when Ross hit the woodwork. Fortunately they still had one outlet in young Bassett on the right wing. The teenager continued to deceive his marker and his acceleration off the mark was quite exceptional. His contribution ultimately proved decisive as the *Free Post* described: 'The backs, who had been having a high old time of it, suddenly cleared their lines, and the forwards, who had been lying in wait, darted off like greyhounds. Ere the North End could reach them they were at the opposite end nearly. Wilson touched over to Bassett, who, in turn, passed to Woodhall, and the trick was done in a twinkling, a splendid screw kick by SPRY sending the ball against the upright from whence it rolled through.'

With only seven minutes remaining, captain Bayliss ordered three of his forwards to augment the Albion defence and they comfortably held out. A final telegram was immediately despatched to an anxious waiting crowd in West Bromwich High Street. *The Free Press* reporter wrote: 'When the final message conveying the news of the victory was made known, the cheering and shouting was beyond description, the vast crowd throwing up hats and sticks and indulging in almost every manifestation of pleasure. Others rushed around mad with excitement to acquaint their friends with the victory, and until a late hour the streets were thronged with people, fireworks being let off in several places in the town.'

Meanwhile back at the Oval, Captain Bayliss with the Cup, Pearson with the trophy lid plus any other Albion players who could be found were carried shoulder high by supporters around the pavilion. The young lads of West Bromwich were bringing home the national Cup. The final word should go to the star performer Billy Bassett: "I remember being mobbed by eager admirers as I strove to find my way to the pavilion. I was very proud."

v Aston Villa 3-0
FA Cup Final. Att: 32,710
19 March 1892

Albion	Aston Villa	Referee
Reader	Warner	J.C. Clegg (Sheffield)
Nicholson	Evans	
McCulloch	Cox	
Reynolds	D. Devey	
Perry	Cowan	
Groves	Baird	
Bassett	Athersmith	
McLeod	J. Devey	
Nicholls	Dickson	
Pearson	Campbell	
Geddes	Hodgetts	

THE 1892 Albion side embraced the latest fashion of looking further afield for talent. The first-team continued to be dominated by West Bromwich men though others came from Oswestry and Blackburn and three were Scottish. The senior players were aged just 26. Albion all time great Billy Bassett was an England star, Groves and Captain Perry had also represented their country while new signing John 'Baldy' Reynolds had gone one better, playing for both England and Ireland. Despite this wealth of talent, Albion had struggled in the League. Their success in the Cup came as a welcome relief.

Aston Villa were overwhelming favourites to lift the trophy. In the League, they'd battered the Throstles 5-1 and 3-0 in addition to an 8-2 hammering in a friendly. As a result, a Villa supporter wrote to the *Birmingham Gazette* sharing his opinion that it was a sheer waste of time and money for Villa to have to travel down to London. Villa had a dinner planned after the game with instructions that a silver salver should be placed in front of the Chairman – presumably to accommodate the FA Cup.

The Albion team were despatched to Enville for special training. This was actually the normal mindless combination of running, walking, lifting weights and skipping with the welcome addition of visits to the famous

Droitwich Spa Baths. They even had a visit from members of the Wolves squad, eager to offer their best wishes – and presumably to better understand what a proper football team looked like!

The Cup final was the last at Kennington Oval as the cricket club were increasingly fearful of large football crowds. Of the 32,000 crowd, it is estimated that at least 3,500 people got in without paying. A further 4,500 were locked outside. Some fans even perched on the famous 100ft high gasometer for a clear view. Such was the crush that many of the 20-deep rows of spectators only saw the ball when it was in the air. Nevertheless, the *Weekly News* reported: 'The Villa supporters were in high glee. It was only a question of just going onto the field as a matter of necessity.'

For the first time in the FA Cup that season, Charlie Perry lost the toss. Villa chose to play with the wind at their backs. The Birmingham side made the most of this slight advantage by piling into the attack. Joe Reader in the Albion goal was quickly called into action, yet it was the hard-pressed Baggies who struck first with only seven minutes played. The *Central Somerset Gazette* describes the move: 'Bassett and McLeod went full pace towards the Villa goal. The neatness of their short passing was stirring to watch. Bassett middled hard, and the ball passing the centre forward (Nicholls) was banged through the goal by GEDDES.' There was a roar of 'surprised cheers from all sides.'

Irritated, Villa resumed their siege. Albion's half-back line in which Reynolds was quite superb completely blotted out several of the Villa forwards but the Birmingham team were still finding some routes to goal. Reader remained formidable. 'Harder to be passed than a policeman on a State occasion', opined the same Somerset journalist. The keeper rode his luck when a shot thudded against his crossbar and a Villa goal was disallowed because an indirect free kick passed Reader without touching anybody.

The Baggies hung on grimly, looking for opportunities to hit back. Midway through the half, Bassett was their outlet, steaming past his marker and crossing for Geddes. The Villa keeper hesitated. Belatedly, he parried Geddes's effort only for the ball to drop kindly for NICHOLLS to tap home.

Back came Villa but once again the chocolate and blues hit a striped wall. As the players left the field for refreshments, the Baggies had a two-goal lead yet boasted only one corner and a handful of incursions into Villa territory.

Any hope of a Villa comeback was completely flattened by a third Albion goal. Baldy REYNOLDS shot from fully 40 yards; keeper Warner misjudged the flight and the ball zipped past him. 'Some of the most execrable goal-keeping ever witnessed', thundered the *Birmingham Daily Post*. The Villa keeper was not to be forgiven. All the windows in his pub were broken and amidst allegations of match-fixing, he was transferred and eventually emigrated.

Meanwhile, the Albion side were content to defend their lead for the rest of the match, mentally preparing for the celebrations. A 3-0 victory was quite sensational.

Because of the crush, the cup was presented to Charlie Perry inside the club pavilion. The Albion party then proceeded to a celebratory dinner at the Criterion Hotel. Billy Bassett was clear who deserved credit for the victory: "I have rarely seen any finer half-back work than Reynolds, Charlie Perry and Groves showed in this final. Many excuses were made for the Villa's defeat, but I think it is generally conceded now that the wonderful play of the Albion half-backs was the deciding factor." Bassett modestly overlooked his own contribution. The *Athletic News* noted that 'he dribbled around like a hare.'

The Albion players left Euston station just before midnight, arriving back in West Bromwich at 3.30am. Despite the ridiculous hour, some 600 supporters welcomed the Cup Winners home.

On the following Monday afternoon, the players toured West Bromwich in a charabanc, starting from George Salters, the club's spiritual home and continuing through the streets to the Star and Garter Hotel where the host entertained them to tea.

The following day, the MP for West Bromwich paid for a dinner for both first and second teams at the Masonic Hall. Councillor Cheshire gave every player a bonus equivalent to six weeks' wages. The dinner was followed by a torchlight procession by the team, a fireworks display and yet another banquet staged by the West Bromwich Poultry Society. In that era at least, WBA knew how to celebrate their achievements.

v Lincoln City 2-1
Att: 6,000
22 April 1911

Albion	Lincoln City	Referee
Pearson	Fern	H. Dale (Manchester)
Smith	Jackson	
Pennington	Wilson	
McNeal	Robson	
Waterhouse	Comnie	
Manners	Wield	
Wright	Haycock	
Thompson	Garrity	
Brewer	Reid	
Buck	Barrell	
Lloyd	Yule	

SINCE 1904, Albion had struggled to escape from the clutches of Division Two. They'd finished third one season, fourth twice and fifth once, none of which were of any value in an era of the first two clubs being promoted and without any play-offs. In truth, the Baggies nearly folded in 1908 due to debts. A takeover led by Billy Bassett was to turn the club around. Money was predictably in short supply so the new-look club was one of the youngest ever Albion sides with half the team having moved up from junior football. The re-shaped Baggies did battle with Bolton and Chelsea at the top of the table. Before the three Easter matches in mid-April, WBA were third. However, Chelsea faltered badly over Easter and so as the young Black Countrymen set off for a marathon train trek to darkest Lincolnshire, the road to promotion was suddenly clear. Albion were top but both opponents had a game in hand. Secretary-manager Fred Everiss had had a particularly busy week. As well as preparing for four matches in eight days, he'd somehow found time to get married to regular supporter Clare Smith.

Lincoln were in danger of seeking re-election and thus with their living at stake, their players were highly determined to overcome the promotion hopefuls by whatever means. Garrity and Haycock, both released by Albion, had an additional incentive. Although being billed locally as 'the greatest League match of the season', the sub-6,000 turnout was disappointing, the heavy rain from noon onwards certainly being a contributory factor.

The Baggies almost managed a dream start in the first minute. Wright left his opponent Wilson for dead and centred for Waterhouse but the forward missed the ball completely. Following up, Manners showed a lack of composure by shooting over the bar. After this alarm, the play was frantic but not very productive. Lincoln were aggressive but uncoordinated. Although Pearson in the Albion goal was twice required to dash out to deal with onrushing forwards, City weren't really worrying peerless Jesse Pennington and his defenders.

It was Albion who made the key breakthrough after 30 minutes. Hard working Albion winger Wright hit the Lincoln crossbar; confused, the City defence made only a half-clearance and Wright nipped in to cross for LLOYD who scored.

Seven minutes later, the Black Country's finest scored again. Again it was Wright doing the damage. He struggled to control a pass from Waterhouse but once he had the ball tamed, he ran straight at the Lincoln defence before squaring to top scorer SID BOWSER. As Sid was all on his own, he had no trouble finding the net. Handshakes all round for the happy Albion team.

Not so, Lincoln. City full back Wilson was convinced his tormentor Wright had handled the ball. Instead of returning the ball to the centre circle, he dropped it where the alleged offence took place. The crowd may have been small but they were determined to have their say. They had already taken a particular dislike to the referee, a Mr Dale, already belligerently claiming that Albion's first goal was offside. They gave Wilson an ovation. The Gentlemen of the Press took a different view. 'He behaved in a very foolish manner', thundered the *Sporting Mail* correspondent.

Although Sid Bowser missed a decent chance, the Albion lads were delighted with their 2-0 lead at half-time. Promotion was looking closer and closer. Maybe they were too delighted and too confident for in the second half, desperate Lincoln were very much on top. Wrote *Birds Eye*: 'I have seldom seen poorer forward play. The members of the Albion attacking line seemed to be satisfied with the result of their efforts in the opening half, for after the interval they were never in the picture.'

Fortunately, the Albion backs were up to the task of defending against an increasingly frantic home side. There were howls of rage with the official each time City forwards were given offside. 'The referee's decisions were the reverse of popular', noted the *Sporting Mail* reporter. Almost every decision given against City was questioned. The match threatened to disintegrate as Lincoln players took out their frustrations on their opponents. There were roars of amusement when Smith, Bowser and Wright were heavily fouled. The latter challenge, predictably by the frustrated Wilson, was particularly unpleasant. Several Lincoln gentlemen in the stand were reported to be dismayed. The *Mail* declared that Wilson should have been dismissed.

Concerned about their furious supporters, club officials moved among them trying to calm the situation down. Albion Director Major Ely also 'offered them some good advice.'

Pearson made one brilliant save from Comnie and Jesse Pennington made two key interceptions but otherwise the visitors were coping well in a difficult situation. However, with just five minutes to go, Lincoln forward REID received a cross from the left and beat Pearson from close quarters. Naturally, the Red Imps now threw everything at the Baggies in the remaining minutes, with a foaming mob backing them. The Albion gallantly held their thin blue and white line. Behind them a blue line of Police had arrived to protect the referee.

Time ran out for Lincoln with Albion doubly grateful for the points which left them top of the table and, more practically, to get off the pitch. City supporters were holding an impassioned demonstration against the referee.

To dodge the mob, Mr Dale ran across fields behind the ground. The supporters, who had declared they wanted to duck him in the local stream, gave chase but he had sufficient lead to escape.

When the successful but slightly worried Albion party left the ground, there were still some noisy individuals in front of the dressing room. Fortunately, the Police protected Albion's retreat to the train station. With Bolton and Chelsea's game in hand being against each other, the Baggies were now just one game away from promotion.

Lincoln lost all their remaining matches but their application for re-election was successful.

v Huddersfield Town 1-0
Att: 30,135
29 April 1911

Albion	Huddersfield Town	Referee
Pearson	Roose	T. Garner (Barnsley)
Joe Smith	Taylor	
Pennington	Bullock	
Baddeley	Beaton	
Waterhouse	Hall	
McNeal	Bartlett	
Wollaston	Blackburn	
Bowser	Howie	
Thompson	Richardson	
Buck	McAuley	
Lloyd	Gee	

THE BAGGIES' hard fought victory over Lincoln extended their sequence to ten wins and two draws in their previous thirteen games. They'd scored 27 goals in those games and beaten both Blues and Wolves. Despite their fine form, the youthful Baggies were only just keeping their noses in front of rivals Bolton and Chelsea, who both had a game in hand. By happy coincidence, their extra fixture was against each other in midweek, prior to the last round of League matches. Bolton beat a Chelsea side missing several key players through injury. As a result, Wanderers headed the table on goal average. It also meant that Albion only needed a point to secure promotion. But a better result for WBA than for Bolton on the last day would guarantee a bigger prize – the Championship.

Among the 30,000 spectators on a warm afternoon at the Hawthorns were two judges. Justice Ridley and Justice Bucknik were warmly applauded (presumably just in case) when they took their seats in the main stand. The turnout was predictably the largest of the campaign, a huge increase on the 6,000 for Stockport in February or the 7,700 for Barnsley in mid-March.

Winger Harry Wright immediately picked up where he left off at Sincil Bank, tormenting his full back and directing a stream of accurate crosses into the box. Amos Lloyd on the opposite wing was doing likewise.

Huddersfield's Roose, the Welsh International goalkeeper and his defenders were under heavy pressure. One of their number, Taylor, was loudly accused of handling the ball in the penalty box. However referee Garner was unimpressed with the claim.

The Huddersfield defenders did have the advantage of being larger than their youthful opponents which helped greatly in aerial battles. Freddie Buck came closest to a precious Albion goal with a fast, low shot which hit the side netting. The one-way traffic continued with WBA forcing a string of corners.

After half an hour, centre forward Thompson was crudely pushed by Bullock in the box. 'Bullock', or something similar his team-mates darkly muttered. Penalty! Coolly, FREDDIE BUCK stepped up and just about squeezed the ball under Roose from the spot, 'to the accompaniment of cheering.' It was Buck's fifth penalty that season and by far his most important. The Baggies had one hand on the Championship.

Not satisfied with a single-goal lead, the Baggies continued to pour forward seeking to create more chances. Their style according to the *Argus* was 'clear and crisp'. From one corner won by Thompson, Buck sailed in to make clear contact with the ball. There was a roar of "Goal!" from the crowd but the ball missed the post by inches. The Yorkshire team's defenders got through an enormous amount of work and repeatedly were forced into errors. Roose made one marvellous save from Thompson, however the Welsh custodian was helpless when Sid Bowser rose unchallenged in front of him but directed his header inches wide of the post.

Without a second goal to secure the game and the Championship, both team and their supporters became increasingly nervous. Their attacks dried up and Huddersfield came into the game more and more.

As the Yorkshiremen sought an equaliser, they created a couple of nervous moments late in the game. Firstly, Albion keeper Pearson needed to make a judicious clearance and moments later he reacted splendidly after the normally immaculate Jesse Pennington had made a rare mistake. In a way Pearson was returning the favour, as earlier in a rare attack a Huddersfield forward had got past him only for Pennington to save the day with a timely boot. The Albion defenders up to then had generally dealt very well with the Huddersfield forward line and notably Gee, their best attacker.

Just as at Lincoln, the Albion defence were preserving a result for the team as the final minutes clicked away. Thankfully, unlike Lincoln, there was no late goal from the opposition. Predictably, there was a pitch invasion at the final whistle with the players having great difficulty in reaching the dressing room safely.

The *Argus* summed up the post-match scene: 'Like a wave, the crowd swept around the grandstand, and, amid an almost indescribable scene of enthusiasm and hilarious joy, the Albion players were fetched from the dressing room to mount the stand and face volley after volley of cheers. It was a scene the like of which had never been witnessed at the ground before.' Two of Albion's senior players, Freddie Buck and Jesse Pennington, spoke on behalf of the team. According to local reports, 'they had a splendid reception.'

For Billy Bassett, who'd invested his reputation and money in reviving the stricken club, promotion was a marvellous payback. He too was 'invited' to make a speech. The Chairman took the opportunity to respond to the critics who had consistently claimed WBA didn't want promotion. "The Albion team showed today that they are keen on reaching the First League," he said, adding he hoped that "some of the people who had been saying the club were satisfied with Second Division football would now remain silent."

Curiously, *Sporting Mail* scribe E.W. Cox reported from Merseyside where thousands of Liverpool fans stayed on at Anfield to catch end-of-season football results from around the country. 'It was gratifying to hear with what pleasure the success of the Albion was received. Ever since Albion's glory days of the 1880s, they have kept a grip on public sentiments. I honestly believe there was no more popular victory in the country than that achieved at the Hawthorns.'

In the end, Albion's victory wasn't necessary as both Bolton and Chelsea lost their respective games. But Champions win matches and Albion were now worthy Champions.

Two days later, Black Country people had an opportunity to properly show appreciation for the achievements of their local club. The Champions of Division Two left the Dartmouth Hotel at 6pm for a celebratory trophy-waving open coach drive around West Bromwich and Smethwick.

v Chelsea 4-0

Att: 35,668
1 May 1920

Albion	Chelsea	Referee
Pearson	Molyneux	F.A. Freemantle (Retford)
Smith	Bettridge	
Pennington	Harrow	
Richardson	Dickie	
Bowser	Logan	
McNeal	Wilding	
Crisp	Ford	
A. W. Smith	Dale	
Morris	Cock	
Gregory	Sharp	
Bentley	McNeill	

THE MASSIVE silver Championship trophy, uniquely decorated with blue and white was prominently displayed in the centre of the grandstand. As Jesse Pennington led his team onto the pitch amid a cacophony of cheering, the Championship flag was hoisted by the club chairman for the one and only time over the Hawthorns. This was Albion's most visibly successful League match.

Far more than just one match in truth, this was simply the Baggies' most successful season. The Black Country had striven to return to normality after the horrors of World War One. There was rampant unemployment, a fatal flu pandemic and tens of thousands of mentally and physically broken men. Amidst all the pain and anguish, West Bromwich Albion provided a blissful escape from reality. Even the setting had changed slightly as WBA had invested money in their ground. All pre-war advertisements were removed and new solid crush barriers were installed. The Smethwick End was now covered in this revamped 50,000 capacity arena.

Nearly all the club's best players such as goalscorer Fred Morris, goalkeeper Hubert Pearson and the incomparable Jesse Pennington survived the war and returned to the Hawthorns. Albion added new young talent such as Tommy Magee to their squad. The combination of old and new was devastating. Right from the first game they jockeyed for top position in the League. By December, they'd established a firm grip on first place and were to remain there for the rest of the season. Notts County were memorably hammered 8-0 while 5 went in the net of Blackburn Rovers (twice) and Everton. Once three points out of the four needed to win the League were secured in two matches against nearest rival Burnley in March, there was no doubt where the title was headed. A 4-0 defeat of Bradford Park Avenue in April secured the Championship. A fortnight later, Albion scored their 100th League goal which equalled the League record. After a 2-0 defeat at third-place Chelsea, the stage was set fair for a spectacular celebratory last match of the season – a return fixture against the West London side.

A decent 35,668 crowd (though only the fourth largest of the season) assembled to properly salute their League Champions and hopefully to see more records tumble. An Albion goal would set a new record for goals scored in a single season. In addition, prolific marksman Fred Morris needed two goals to beat the First Division scoring record currently held by Bert Freeman. Fred had already amassed 37 goals, including 5 against Notts County and scored in 10 consecutive fixtures.

The Baggies were determined to put on a show to cement their place in League history. Although Chelsea showed numerous delightful touches with their forward, Cock, particularly prominent, the Baggies needed only 17 minutes to net their 101st goal and with it exceed Sunderland's 100-goal record. Gregory received a long pass from Morris and lobbed the ball into the penalty box. Smith's shot was intercepted but the ball dropped handily on the penalty spot. The onrushing McNEAL happily thumped the ball past the appallingly-named Molyneux.

Not wanting to be overrun by their rampant opponents, Chelsea circled their goal with defenders and hung on grimly. Naturally, the Baggies needed time to prise open a route to goal. There was some amusement when Jesse Pennington passed back to his goalkeeper with considerable force. Pearson hung on desperately. History sadly doesn't record whether Pennington was merely being playful. The Albion defender was so on top of his opponent, Chelsea's lone forward, Cock, that the Hawthorns crowd took pity on the Londoner. "Let Cock have a kick," they sniggered aloud with much glee.

Chelsea's frustrations were enhanced when their ardent appeals for a penalty were refused. This after their man Dale had made contact with Albion's Bowser in the penalty box. Chelsea became positively apoplectic when the Baggies scored their second early in the second half. GREGORY headed the ball just over the line from a crisp centre from Crisp. Molyneux believed he'd stopped the ball crossing the line but no-one was going to pay any attention to him.

Their sense of grievance was such that by the time Chelsea had recovered their equilibrium, they were 3-0 down. A.W. SMITH did the damage with a beautiful drive into the far corner of the net.

Cock forced a save from Albion goalkeeper Pearson but the rest of his team-mates had pretty much given up the fight. The goals record was broken again seven minutes later when Crisp knocked down Gregory's high centre to the waiting BENTLEY.

With one record secure, the Albion team did their best to set up Morris for the two goals he needed but the West London side were wise to this and multi-man marked him. With the rest of his team-mates refusing to take any other route to goal, the match became quite farcical. Unfortunately, Morris was having 'one of those days' and was quite unable to shoot straight when he was able to elude mass marking. The ever proud Cock almost showed him how it was done when he pounced on a poor pass by McNeal but big Pearson foiled his attempt.

As the minutes ebbed away, sections of the crowd massed on the edge of the pitch. As soon as they were able, all the players belted towards the safety of the dressing rooms. The slower ones were caught, hoisted high and paraded proudly around the Hawthorns as human trophies until they could make their escape.

In a hugely proud moment for WBA, Football League President John McKenna presented the veteran Albion captain Jesse Pennington with the Championship trophy. The Albion Chairman insisted this fine player should receive the trophy rather than himself, which was customary. McKenna was fulsome in his praise of the Baggies: "It gives me great pleasure to present Albion with this trophy, which has been won by so many great teams – but never has the Championship been won by a more brilliant team."

v Birmingham 2-1
FA Cup Final Att: 92,406
25 April 1931

Albion	Birmingham	Referee
Pearson	Hibbs	A.H. Kingscott
Shaw	Liddell	
Trentham	Barkas	
Magee	Cringan	
W. Richardson	Morrall	
Edwards	Leslie	
Glidden	Briggs	
Carter	Crosbie	
W.G. Richardson	Bradford	
Sandford	Gregg	
Wood	Curtis	

ALBION'S FIRST ever visit to the twin towers was earned the hard way despite only being obliged to play one side from the top division (Portsmouth). Stubborn Charlton defied the Black Country maestros for 270 minutes while their other 3 opponents, Everton, Spurs and Wolverhampton finished first, third and fourth in the Second Division. None of them were worthy of the description of patsies … well OK, maybe one of them. Arguably the toughest assignment was knocking out runaway League leaders Everton including Dixie Dean in the semi-final at a very muddy Old Trafford. The Albion goal was under siege for most of the match with the Baggies stealing a victory with a freak W.G. Richardson goal.

Their Cup final opponents would be the downbeat neighbours, First Division Birmingham. Naturally such a clash fascinated the whole area. Team photographs and blue and white ribbons for both teams adorned hundreds of shops and houses.

Both sets of supporters travelled to London by train, often the same one. In addition to the regular service, there were 48 special trains laid on from central Birmingham stations. Second city trains were arriving into Paddington every 12 minutes on Cup final day. It was unfortunate that the supporters' special day was dampened by such wet and miserable weather.

Rain fell all day and although 1930s people were a tough bunch, they could have done without such a deluge.

Wembley ticket touts had a poor afternoon, unable to shift dozens of tickets even at the cover price while getting very wet. What a shame. The logic appeared to be that all the Midlands-based travellers had bought tickets in advance, even though club allocations were pitifully small. The Baggies were given just 7,500 tickets to distribute between 80,000+ applicants.

The *Daily Express* correspondent confessed that he could not tell the difference between Albion and Birmingham supporters at Wembley: 'Experts, I am told, could sort them out, but they were all the same to me.' In fairness to the no doubt London-based reporter, hours of standing on uncovered terraces under heavy precipitation adds uniformity to all spectators. The conditions meant the noise level was lower than in past years but stoically everyone stayed until the very end, bar a dozen fair-weathers in the grandstand.

On such a heavy surface the match was all about slogging out a result rather than passing football. The Bluenoses thought they had found the net first but the referee disagreed, deciding that Gregg was offside when he headed home from a Clingan free kick. He was in a very small minority with that decision.

It was Albion who took the lead midway through the first half. Carter spotted top scorer W.G. RICHARDSON making a run and provided a fine pass. W.G.'s shot was a bit of a dog's dinner but it was sufficient to defeat Blues' England keeper Hibbs.

Birmingham ought to have read the Wembley script – clubs who go behind in the Cup final lose. They had the temerity to challenge that rule by equalising. In the 59th minute from a Curtis cross, JOE BRADFORD hit the ball with depressing accuracy past Pearson in the Albion goal. The Albion defenders claimed offside but after the earlier incident, the referee wasn't buying it. Albion's senior professional and man-of-the-match-elect Tommy Magee was unhappy: "Gregg was a yard offside – he was in front of me and I was the last Albion defender, apart from the goalkeeper."

The Baggies made an instant riposte. Joe Carter: "When Joe Bradford had put the scores level, I imagined that, for a few minutes at any rate, Blues would be a little excited and off their guard. I said to our chaps, 'now is our time' and off we went and pretty soon we had recaptured the lead." Pretty soon was less than a minute. Three Albion forwards – Carter, Sandford and W.G. Richardson – dribbled their way through the still celebrating Blues ranks and it was RICHARDSON who applied the coup de grace. Hibbs got his fingers to the ball but couldn't prevent the goal.

Supporter W.J. O'Reilly will never forget that moment: "To see the Albion players passing and re-passing the ball, drawing nearer and nearer, bigger and bigger until Hibbs dashed out to dive at Richardson's feet, only for Billy to trick him and walk the ball into goal, was my biggest thrill in watching football for 65 years."

Most teams who fight back against the odds to level, only to concede again, would be flattened. Birmingham *were* flattened. Only in the last five frantic minutes could they exert any pressure on the Albion goal. Pearson was forced to tip over from Gregg's powerful drive and from the resulting corner the goalkeeper had to punch away another shot. The Brummies got a little close for comfort and the soggy Albion side were very grateful that time ran out for their opponents.

Both sides resembled an extended mud wrestling team, spattered in the brown stuff. The *Daily Express* correspondent noted: 'The dirtiest of them all was Magee, the right half-back. Magee's dirt was the blackest of blacks. It covered his shorts and concealed half his jersey. In fact, he was the blackest-looking footballer I have ever seen.' Ever the joker, Tommy was heard to ask "Has it been raining?" as he lined up in front of the Duke of Gloucester to receive his winners' medal. Said the Duke (a late substitute for the Prince of Wales) admiringly: "You boys have been wonderful." The words were surprisingly well chosen as the Albion side, with the youngest average age of any Cup final side to date, had been regularly called 'the team of boys'.

Meanwhile, Birmingham had properly bedded in their culture of not winning anything. To this day, they've maintained this tradition with startling consistency, cleverly losing in embarrassing fashion whenever a trophy became a bit too close.

v Charlton Athletic 3-2

Att: 52,415

2 May 1931

Albion	Charlton Athletic	Referee
Pearson	Robertson	W.E. Russell (Swindon)
Finch	Smith	
Shaw	Langford	
Magee	Pitcairn	
W. Richardson	Pritchard	
Edwards	Pugsley	
Glidden	Wyper	
Carter	McKay	
WG Richardson	Astley	
Sandford	McLeod	
Wood	Horton	

SOMETIMES THE same opposition pops up time and time again in one season to be a damn nuisance. During 1978/79, Leeds United got in the way seven times while in more recent times Wolves met Albion five times during 2007/08. Back in 1930/31 such regular clashes were less likely with only two competitions yet Charlton and Albion battled three times in the FA Cup as well as twice in the Second Division. In the Cup, Albion recovered from a two goal deficit at the Hawthorns, from one goal behind in the Valley replay and again in the second replay before finally winning 3-1.

To be sure of securing promotion behind champions Everton to add to their Wembley triumph, the Baggies had to win both their remaining League matches.

But the fixtures were separated by only 45 hours and this for a team leg-weary from winning the FA Cup final on a sea of mud. The first hurdle was achieved with a narrow 1-0 win at Stoke early Thursday evening (who mentioned damn nuisances?). It was a tense, wearing night with Trentham a limping passenger and Magee enduring a heavy cold. That barrier just about clambered over, there was one more hurdle to overcome – taking on the stubborn courage of Charlton yet again, this time at the Hawthorns.

Great Depression or no Great Depression, Black Country folk were determined to be at this match with over 52,000 squeezing into the Hawthorns. The Wolves match apart, the gate was double the season average.

For Charlton this was a routine end-of-season fixture but their players were up for another fight. In theory, a draw would suffice for Albion providing their only rivals, Spurs, didn't win 4-0 or better against Burnley (whom they'd already beaten 8-1 earlier in the season).

Any idea of an easy afternoon at the Hawthorns was wiped away by DAI ASTLEY scoring for the Londoners after only eight minutes. Still, Albion had done it before and would do it again surely? Both Wood and the normally deadly W.G. Richardson shot over. Glidden hit the bar and Sandford hit the post for the Baggies before the blessed relief of a TEDDY SANDFORD leveller. The Albion man neatly lobbed goalkeeper Robertson who had rashly strayed from his line trying to reach an Albion corner.

Surely Albion would now stroll to victory? *No!* Charlton were determined to fight and found the net for the second time, again from the now infuriating ASTLEY. His finish from a Horton cross was uncomfortably similar to his first goal. The Baggies had been level for only three minutes and were now obliged to fight back from a goal deficit against the Londoners for the fifth time that season.

Incredibly, WBA only needed two minutes to complete that fifth comeback. Winger Wood's cross was missed by W.G. Richardson but TOMMY GLIDDEN found the far corner of the net. Tens of thousands of caps were launched skywards. The equaliser arrived just the right side of the half-time whistle.

Uniquely at the Hawthorns for a promotion decider, the crowd had a trophy to admire at half-time. Injured defender Bert Trentham proudly carried the FA Cup all round the ground, under the watchful eye of a solitary policeman. There's a famous picture of the Albion man, wearing a large cap and what appears to be stripy socks holding the FA Cup up to the massed ranks of supporters. As was the custom at the time, young boys were huddled together on the running track – all wearing flat caps – and they enjoyed a prime view of the trophy.

Charlton's Astley came desperately close after the re-start to adding to his tally when he was clear through on the Albion goalkeeper. Urged on by the packed crowd, the Baggies pressed Athletic's defence. In the 68th minute, the caps were airborne once again when W.G. RICHARDSON headed home from Glidden's cross. W.G. didn't do a lot of heading but rarely has one header made so much difference to Albion's history.

At last Charlton were getting the message that party poopers were not welcome. They didn't manage another chance in the remaining minutes as the home side only cautiously tried to find a winning goal. As it happened, their only rivals Spurs had lost 1-0 but the news reached the Hawthorns too late to make any difference.

At the end of the game, the massive crowd invaded the pitch and almost overwhelmed the stragglers among the victorious side as they scrambled for safety. A sea of people engulfed the turf. They were vociferous in their demands that the team should return and be recognised. The double-winners duly made an appearance along the front row of the main stand.

Chairman Billy Bassett did his best to offer tributes over the raucous noise, confessing that "it's one of the proudest days of my life." He also re-used a phrase much in vogue that term – 'a team of boys' – reflecting the comparatively youthful nature of the players. Captain Tommy Glidden also made a brief speech of thanks. He was normally a man of few words and those at the back of the ground had no chance of hearing his pearls of wisdom so the supporters collectively remained unsatisfied. They waited outside the dressing rooms until the players emerged to catch their trams home. Then any player was considered fair game to chair around like royalty. Teddy Sandford who resided only yards from the ground was literally taken home by happy supporters.

History doesn't record what accolade W.G. Richardson, Albion's top goalscorer, received. His 24 strikes included so many key goals in the last week of the season. In barely a week, he had scored twice to win the Cup at Wembley, grabbed a crucial winner at Stoke and then confirmed promotion with his header. It was an amazing week for him and his club. The Cup and promotion double remains unique to WBA. No other club has ever matched this spectacular achievement.

v Leicester City 3-0
Att: 34,585
5 May 1949

Albion	Leicester City	Referee
Sanders	Major	(Unknown)
Pemberton	Jelly	
Millard	Scott	
Ryan	Harrison	
Vernon	Plummer	
Hood	Johnston	
Elliott	Griffiths	
Kennedy	King	
Walsh	Lee	
Barlow	Chisholm	
Smith	Adam	

SINCE THE end of the War, Albion had struggled to escape upwards from the Second Division. Dave Walsh was finding the net regularly so the 'goals for' column took care of itself. The total goals conceded needed attention and led to Albion finishing seventh two seasons in a row. But in the summer of 1948, Albion's first ever manager Jack Smith took over from the retiring secretary Fred Everiss. The enthusiastic incomer boldly added promising youngsters like Ray Barlow and Joe Kennedy to his squad. This, combined with a new found team spirit and a master plan to turn every away match into a short holiday, led to significantly more goals scored than conceded with 16 League clean sheets by the end of April.

Albion crucially hit form during the run-in securing 17 points out of a possible 22 just as League leaders Southampton were faltering. In their final home game, 32,000 turned out for a 2-0 defeat of Barnsley. Results elsewhere meant one win from their remaining two matches guaranteed promotion back to the big time after 11 years' absence. Convinced promotion was secure, Mrs Jones of Langley made a lavishly decorated blue and white 'Up the Baggies' cake. She delivered the 4lb gift to the Hawthorns just after the players had departed for the East Midlands.

The Baggies had a date with Leicester City who had creditably just played in the FA Cup Final (losing to Wolves) but required a point to stay in the Division. City had two major concerns. Firstly, following an injury in the Cup final their midfield inspiration Don Revie was still in a hospital bed. Secondly, with Leicester having played and won the previous day at Bury with the same team, the City first-team were hardly at their freshest.

The importance of the match fired the imagination despite being a Thursday afternoon kick-off. The area ground to a halt as three separate queues, each eight to ten people-wide stretched for a quarter of a mile. There was never any hope of squeezing such a vast crowd into pokey Filbert Street. Predictably tens of thousands were locked out but with no other way of keeping in touch, they opted to stay as close to Filbert Street as possible. The sheer numbers created danger, notably when a gate collapsed and an estimated 3,000 more supporters rushed into a ground already declared full. Very fortunately, there were no reports of injuries.

Alongside regular centre-forward Dave Walsh, Albion played Ray Barlow and Joe Kennedy up front, a role neither youngster were familiar with but both were tall and the manager decreed they would make an impact. He was to be proved right.

The first blow was so nearly struck by Leicester. Their striker, Griffiths, stretched to reach a cross from his winger, Lee. He succeeded in only getting his toe to the ball to deflect it onto the Albion bar. When the ball rebounded, a whole melee of players from either side kicked wildly and inaccurately at it before finally an Albion boot walloped the ball clear. It was a clear sign of nervous tension.

Fortunately for the Albion, they smoothly passed their way to the other end of the pitch and promptly took the lead. From a Reg Ryan free kick, young Kennedy made the most of his spring-heeled skills to remarkably rise above the Leicester goalkeeper and set up DAVE WALSH for an easy tap-in. The relief was immense and the goal uplifted the whole Albion side.

Within ten minutes young rookie striker KENNEDY coolly headed Albion's second goal from a corner, his first ever in the League. The Baggies could almost taste their promotion drinks while the Leicester side could only feel the desperate fatigue in their limbs. But there was a lot of football still to play. Urged on by their supporters, Leicester rallied and the surety of a two goal advantage began to diminish.

The City manager used his Wembley tactic of swapping positions for five of his team. Just as in the Cup final, the outcome was a more attacking and determined display. This match was not yet done. Albion keeper Jimmy Sanders and his defenders were increasingly hard-pressed but held on doggedly, breaking up Leicester moves. The absence of Revie, so skilled at prizing open defences, was keenly felt.

It was RAY BARLOW who provided ultimate relief. A rare Albion attacking move opened up a surprised Leicester defence and lanky Ray saw his opportunity at the far post. His shot, despite the narrowness of the angle was perfect. Albion had a 3-0 lead and with only 27 minutes remaining everyone knew the game was won.

As the final minutes were played out, Baggies fans stood close to the halfway line, revelling in the atmosphere and the sense of a job very well done. The referee's last whistle came as both a relief and a joy. The handful of 'bobbies' were powerless to resist a full pitch invasion as all the Albion players were hoisted shoulder high and carried in triumph round and round the ground. Albion were back in Division One – a fascinating and novel prospect for so many of their supporters. The train ride back home from Leicester was simply a great place to be.

Albion Chairman Major Wilson Keys admitted that he was "happy to be rejoining old friends, particularly Aston Villa, Birmingham and the Wolves. We are naturally very relieved. It has been an extremely anxious season and I think we can say that nothing has been served on a plate to us." (All three Midlands clubs were quick to send congratulatory telegrams.) Major Keys was quick to add consoling words for Leicester: "Leicester supporters took their defeat handsomely and I admired them for it."

Two days later, weary Leicester got the draw they needed to retain their status but a knackered Albion lost 1-0 at Grimsby thus missing the Championship by one point.

v Newcastle United 7-3

Att: 58,075

7 September 1953

Albion	Newcastle United	Referee
Heath	Simpson	T. Seymour (Wakefield)
Rickaby	Cowell	
Millard	Batty	
Dudley	Scoular	
Dugdale	Brennan	
Barlow	Crowe	
Griffin	Milburn	
Ryan	Davies	
Allen	Keeble	
Nicholls	Hannah	
Lee	Mitchell	

VINTAGE SUPPORTERS insist the 1953/54 Albion team was the best in the club's history. It was based around the exquisite long passing skills of Ray Barlow, the intelligent roaming of striker Ronnie Allen combined with Johnny 'On the Spot' Nicholls's goal poaching instincts. But this was a team with talented individuals from front to back.

This magnificent team were unbeaten in their first eight League games. Indeed, they'd dropped only two points out of the sixteen available and led the Championship race by two points. One of their draws was a 2-2 against Newcastle at the Hawthorns a week earlier. United had already proved to be tough opponents. Yet with 19 goals to their name already, an evening return fixture in Geordie land shouldn't have overly worried the League leaders. After all, in the previous two seasons, the Baggies had triumphed 4-1 and 5-3 in Newcastle.

It should be said that during this era, Newcastle were normally formidable at home. Their team, which included names like 'Wor' Jackie Milburn, is considered to this day as being one of the best Newcastle teams ever. They were at their best in the Cup, reaching the FA Cup final in both 1951 and 1952 (and would follow this with a third appearance in 1955).

It was unfortunate that St James' Park is traditionally the longest and most arduous trip in the country for Albion supporters. Travelling to Newcastle on a Saturday meant an 8am departure from New Street to Derby. Change here for a train to York and just pray that the connection from York to Newcastle would be on time, meaning an arrival in the Geordie nation at 2pm. The return was even worse with a 7pm departure which, assuming smooth connections, meant a 2am arrival back in Birmingham just minutes too late for the hourly all-night bus service. With this fixture being an evening kick-off, returning that evening was impossible. Thus for any supporters determined to travel, Newcatle away would be a two day epic. As the average Albion turnout for a 1950s Saturday match at Newcastle was around 200, the midweek travelling band would be very small indeed.

The Baggies were at full strength for this game. They charged forward early, clearly wanting to repeat the 5-3 scoreline of the previous season. They quickly forced a mistake from a Newcastle defender and only a desperate hack off the line prevented an embarrassing early goal. United's back division were struggling to keep up with the fleet footed and numerous Albion attackers. Ronnie Allen had a goal chalked off for a desperately tight offside decision and the same man hammered the ball against the post. His team-mates were just as unlucky, peppering the Newcastle goal from all directions. Somehow with a third of the game gone, neither side had scored but the Geordies couldn't hold on indefinitely against this one-way tide.

Deservedly, it was RONNIE ALLEN who made the breakthrough, despatching the ball past Simpson from outside the penalty box. Minutes later, the England striker burst through again and although the Newcastle keeper managed to block his shot, he could only divert the ball to the alert NICHOLLS who easily found the net.

Some sides would be delighted with a 2-0 lead and be content to sit back, but not Albion. Still they attacked and they were rewarded with a third goal. The irrepressible ALLEN netted his second, albeit with some help from a defender's leg. Three goals up with the second half still to come.

You might imagine with the eye of a modern intolerant that the home crowd would be furious with both their own team and the irritatingly superior opponents. Not so, as an astonished Stan Rickaby noted: 'The crowd gave us the biggest reception I've ever known away from home. Going off at half-time and coming on again after the interval they simply rose to us – and we were 3-0 up.'

Not surprisingly, cross words were exchanged in the Newcastle dressing room. The United players were transformed. For once, the Baggies were on the back foot. Within just three minutes, KEEBLE had reduced the deficit and the Geordies were in full cry. Newcastle were dominating the middle of the pitch and when BOBBY MITCHELL scored United's second with fully 30 minutes remaining, the handful of Baggies supporters present had every right to be worried.

Just when United thought the game was within their grasp, Albion found another gear. The classic Barlow-Nicholls-Allen triumvirate did the damage culminating in a simple tap-in for JOHNNY NICHOLLS. 2-4 felt more comfortable but their comfort zone was brief. Stung into action, MITCHELL scored again for the Geordies 15 minutes from time. 3-4 and game on. Again.

The Baggies were unfazed and continued to push forward. Just three minutes later NICHOLLS found space in the middle to break through a gap in the Newcastle defence to wrap up his first ever hat-trick in the League. Not surprisingly, he was later to describe this match as "my best game for the Albion." Just 60 seconds later, REG RYAN scored Albion's sixth with a thundering shot. United were finally beaten. Doughty scrappers that they were, they had nothing left to fight back with against the Black Country's finest.

Even in the closing minutes the Baggies were instinctively drawn to the Newcastle goal like moths around a light bulb. FRANK GRIFFIN on the Albion wing zipped past his markers and added Albion's seventh goal – their biggest total away from home since 1946. Even then, Ronnie Allen continued to chase his own well deserved hat-trick and came painfully close. In injury time, he sped single-handedly through the Geordies' shattered defence. To Allen's chagrin, Simpson in the Newcastle goal dashed forward and niftily snatched the ball off his toes.

This extraordinary seven-goal display was worthy only of Champions. That night everyone at St James' had no doubts that they'd seen the next League Champions in action.

v Preston North End 3-2
FA Cup Final. Att: 99,842
1 May 1954

Albion	Preston NE	Referee
Sanders	Thompson	A.W. Luty (West Riding)
Kennedy	Cunningham	
Millard	Walton	
Dudley	Docherty	
Dugdale	Marston	
Barlow	Forbes	
Griffin	Finney	
Ryan	Foster	
Allen	Wayman	
Nicholls	Baxter	
Lee	Morrison	

IN 1954, Wembley was a near-mythical place for Black Country folk, glimpsed only in newspaper pictures, or for the fortunate wealthy few, on a flickering 12-inch TV. Almost two decades and a World War had passed since the Baggies had last played under the twin towers, back in 1935. And soon, as US General McArthur avowed, during the recent global conflict, "they would return".

During the season in question, the Baggies were simply the best; dazzling coruscations of the most skilful, entertaining performers English football had to offer glitter-strewn throughout their team, clear League leaders for much of the season, but overhauled in the run-in by Wolverhampton. This painful slip was not due to lack of morale, but strength-sapping attrition of key players through injuries, and international call-ups (League matches weren't postponed for England games, back then). Albion had the best team all right – but not the best squad. The would-be Double Winners now had but a single target.

With four home Cup draws, and a semi-final against a Third Division side, WBA seemingly had the easier ride to Wembley. Of course, the reality was much harder, notably the last hurdle, when only a late Allen penalty finally defeated Port Vale. Getting tickets were difficult enough for the Villa Park semi – the vigil began at 5pm the previous Saturday – but obtaining tickets for the Final? No priority whatsoever was given to the regulars who'd devotedly travelled the entire length and breadth of Blighty all season, for the cause; Albion simply declared a lottery for the miserly 12,000 allocation. The Post Office reported selling 70,000 Postal Orders within a few days. Albion fan Terry Wills was predictably unlucky, but an impassioned plea to the *Mail* mercifully brought forth a Good Samaritan and he travelled by train for what would be £1.15 in modern currency: "Wembley really was wonderful. To see the anticipation on everyone's face! We were there at the Mecca of football, and most important of all, to see our team attempting to win the most sought after prize in football."

Chris Flanagan, too young to travel, was of a TV-owning family, so he would watch the game alongside every relative who could be crammed into the family living room: "As I sat there in front of the TV clutching my knees, I couldn't think of anything else I'd rather be doing – other than breathing."

Albion, indifferent League form and all, were pitched against a decent Preston side, including one Tom Finney. Worse still, first choice goal-keeper Norman Heath was permanently injured; ditto regular right-back Stan Rickaby. His stand-in would be Kennedy, new to that position and without a Cup match to his name in 15 months.

Preston were perfectly aware how much Ronnie Allen could hurt them, so spent much of the early minutes of the final hurting *him*. ALLEN, being well-used to such treatment, simply concentrated on being in the right place at the right time, and this strategy paid off with a far post tap-in from Lee's left wing cross.

Preston needed seven minutes to equalise via Finney eluding his marker, to set up MORRISON, and were in the ascendancy when Wayman missed a glorious chance from close-in. Albion fought back to create their own chances, but it was Preston who took the lead, and in controversial circumstances. WAYMAN was so outrageously offside that the whole Albion side stopped dead as he walked the ball into the net – and the Preston player was as surprised as anyone that the goal stood. On the terraces, Terry Wills swore fluently in Chinese (vocabulary courtesy of National Service in Hong Kong).

Then it was North End's turn to feel aggrieved. Tommy Docherty baulked Ray Barlow as he charged into the box. Result? A penalty. Barlow confessed later: "I don't think I would have given it."

This was Albion's first ever penalty in a Cup final – no pressure then...Coolly, Ronnie Allen ran forward – only to be halted by the increasingly irritating fusspot in black, who now wanted the ball repositioned. The drama was too much and many, goalkeeper Sanders included, averted their gaze.

Chris Flanagan remembers the incident: "I stopped breathing as Ronnie stepped forward. After the arguments about exactly where the penalty spot was, I started to die quietly. Then Ronnie's successful strike brought me back from the dead." Preston keeper Thompson got very close to stopping ALLEN'S effort, but not close enough. Albion were back in business. "When Thompson touched it, I was in agony. Thank goodness he couldn't hold it," a relieved Allen later said.

Nerves were jangling, both on and off the pitch. Still Finney was being held in check – but Ronnie Allen wasn't. An astute Joe Kennedy through-ball gave him the chance of a hat-trick, but his shot missed by inches.

Only three minutes remained. Kennedy slid the ball forward to FRANK GRIFFIN, who cut in, then squeezed in a shot from a desperately narrow angle – and suddenly, the ball was nestling in the back of the net.

"When it went into the net, I'll swear my heart stood still," said the goalscorer.

Terry Wills recalls the ensuing bedlam: "The Albion contingent around me immediately fled as my heavy wooden rattle went into over-drive. We were nearly there...keep 'em out...kick it anywhere...come on...blow that bloody whistle, ref...for God's sake, has yer watch stopped?!" Then, after a nerve-jangling, rollercoaster 93 minutes, it was all over – and Albion had won the Cup. "There is no prouder sight in football than watching your team showing off the FA Cup," beamed Terry, rattle now silent.

Back in Handsworth, ecstatic Chris Flanagan eagerly awaited the Saturday night specials outside his local newsagent: "I'd been outside Mrs Burton's for ages and ages by the time the pink *Arguses* and the blue *Mails* were chucked over the vans onto the pavement. Me and another kid carried the papers into the shop. A bloke with a squint bought five of each. One and eight pence it cost him."

v Nottingham Forest 5-1
Att: 46,455
28 January 1958

Albion	Nottm Forest	Referee
Sanders	Thomson	(Unknown)
Howe	Ware	
Stuart Williams	Thomas	
Setters	Morley	
Kennedy	McKinlay	
Barlow	Burkitt	
Griffin	Gray	
Whitehouse	Quigley	
Robson	Wilson	
Kevan	Baily	
Horobin	Imlach	

IN THE late 1950s, it was expected that Albion would make progress in the country's number one cup competition. The Baggies had formidable goalscorers in Allen and Kevan in addition to international-quality midfielders and defenders. After all, their Wembley triumph in 1954 was their fourth lifting of the FA Cup, an achievement few clubs could match.

This season, Manchester City were routed 5-1 in the Third Round. In the next round, in front of 58,000 expectant Hawthorns fans (including 15,000 from the East Midlands), newly promoted Nottingham Forest were expected to go the same way. That was until Ronnie Allen twisted his ankle in the first minute on a hard, unyielding pitch. With no substitutes permitted the England star had to carry on as best he could and hope to avoid long term side effects.

Inspired by Bobby Robson and Ray Barlow, the ten men came back from a goal down to set up three second half Albion goals in just four minutes. The limping Ronnie Allen tapped in the third from Horobin's centre, but the East Midlands side pulled a goal back within a minute through Ray Barlow's handball and went on to grab a 3-3 draw and a replay. They'd been fortunate that the home side missed late chances (Allen hit the crossbar in the last minute) and even more fortunate that the great Ronnie Allen wouldn't be fit for a midweek afternoon replay.

Antediluvian supporter Terry Wills had to work hard to persuade his rugby-loving boss to give him the afternoon off. His answer was long in coming and reluctant but it was ultimately positive. With a car still being a luxury item in this era, for supporters such as Terry who were able to travel, the football special which left New Street at 10.30 was their best option. Just over 35p transported you to Nottingham station in 2 hours. Forest supporters were confident their team would win. They were very eager to share that thought with visiting Baggies on the mass plod to the ground. Interest in the match was high with over 46,000 packed in the City Ground. Albion's 1,200 seats sold out within hours though the game was not all-ticket. Ray Barlow chanced to be passing by the ticket queue and was jocularly told: "It's your fault we're here!" (a reference to his handball).

The visitors set the pace creating a series of chances, none of which were taken. Unexpectedly, it was Nottingham who took the lead through WILSON in the 13th minute, an irritatingly easy header that Albion keeper Sanders wrongly assumed would drift wide. Forest supporters invaded the pitch in their excitement, creating a delay of several minutes.

The Albion still had plenty of fight within them. Within ten minutes, from a corner BOBBY ROBSON outjumped a defender to nod home an equaliser. Unfortunately their joy was short-lived. Barely a minute later, hard man Maurice Setters was carried off, writhing on a stretcher with a painful ankle injury. From the onset he had been the rock on which numerous Forest attacks had floundered, famously getting his retaliation in first. With 57 minutes remaining, the Baggies had to continue with just ten men.

Stand-in centre-forward Bobby Robson reverted to a more defensive position, then commonly known as right-half. There were so many gaps to fill and the England man did his best to plug the lot. Famous cartoonist Norman Edwards later described his position as: 'centre-right-forward-half-full-back'.

Remarkably, Albion proceeded to take the lead through FRANK GRIFFIN's right-foot shot. Utilising the language of the period: "Come on the ten men, you can do it," chorused their supporters.

Half-time offered the tiring ten a chance to regroup. In the second half, they came again, with WHITEHOUSE, who'd replaced Allen in the side, sliding home the Baggies' third after a fine through ball from Derek

Kevan. There was never a doubt from that moment on that the ten man Baggies were going to beat a full strength side from their own Division on their own pitch.

The ball wasn't just passed around to kill time. As the *Birmingham Mail* reported: '...slowly the greatness of this Albion side blossomed in front of us. Every man tackled, chased and shot like men inspired. But most incredible of all they persisted in playing rich dreamy soccer in these back to the walls conditions. An incredible sight...men playing short balls inside their own six yard box. But the shock gradually wore off, as never once did they falter, never once was a ball wasted.'

Concerted chants were virtually unheard during this period yet the jubilant Black Country travelling men managed a lusty "We want four". And four they got as, remarkably, DEREK KEVAN added to the ten men's total from twenty yards. Forest understandably lost heart after this final straw setback. Amid a revised chorus, this time "We want five", Forest defender Ware conceded a penalty by chopping down Griffin. DON HOWE duly obliged with the visitors' fifth.

Home supporters, heads bowed, were pouring out of the ground long before the final whistle. Although the Baggies couldn't quite meet supporters' demands who naturally now wanted a round half-dozen goals, such was the magnificence of the display that dozens of raincoat-wearing Albion supporters invaded the pitch at the end.

The Forest manager Billy Walker was gracious in defeat: "I'm not complaining. I saw the Cup Winners today." The Sheffield United manager Joe Mercer (United would play the winners in Round Five) was rueful: "The best performance I have ever seen in my life and I had to bring my team to see it." Writing in the *Birmingham Mail*, Eric Woodward concluded: 'I salute a wonderful display. And I repeat that whatever happens on the rocky road to Wembley ahead; their display will never be forgotten.'

Pehaps the last word should be given to whoever wrote the notice in the dust on Albion's coach: 'Dear Joe [Mercer] Gone to river to drown myself...'

v Aston Villa 1-1

Att: 48,261
29 April 1959

Albion	Aston Villa	Referee
Potter	Sims	Mr Rosekilly
Howe	Lynn	
Williams	Winton	
Robson	Crowe	
Kennedy	Dugdale	
Barlow	Saward	
Hogg	Myerscough	
Jackson	Dixon	
Allen	Hitchens	
Kevan	Wylie	
Campbell	McParland	

A STON VILLA had flirted deliciously with one of the two relegation spots for most of the season. Happy days! Their major problem came away from home with the Villains securing only three wins and a pair of saggy draws all season. They weren't much better at Villa Park. The Baggies beat the claret and blue also-rans 4-1 (their first win in Witton since the war) as befitting a team who were in the top 6 all season.

The relegation quicksand sucked furiously at claret and blue legs. They were unable to pull clear before the season's final game which happily was at the Hawthorns. Villa and Manchester City were level on points after 41 games. Only a win for Villa and defeat for Manchester City at home to Leicester would guarantee survival for the Brummies. Anything else meant the vagaries of goal average came into play. Curiously, the Hawthorns fixture kicked off 15 minutes earlier than the Manchester City v Leicester game. The Baggies were the form team with only one defeat in their previous nine matches.

Pre-match press speculation suggested that Albion didn't seriously want to relegate a local club. Their logic was based on money (as was normal practice during the period – Albion received a half share of the huge gate at Villa Park) and travel (most away trips were tiring train epics whereas Villa was theoretically walkable). Albion supporters furiously rubbished these suggestions. We owed them one following a particularly maddening FA Cup semi-final defeat two years earlier. A virtual ten man West Bromwich side had lost to a single breakaway goal despite laying siege to the Brummies' goal for the whole game. Furthermore, there was talent money at stake (a payout to players whose team finished in the first few places of the First Division) so the stars in stripes had an extra incentive to win.

But why should an Albion team ever need an incentive to put one over AVFC – the real old enemy? Certainly this Baggies team tore into their nervous visitors from the first whistle with tackles flying in all directions. Albion supporters screamed "foul!" with every Villa challenge. They had good cause with both Alec Jackson and Derek Hogg needing treatment after making painful contact with ill-judged Villa boots. The atmosphere was gut-wrenchingly tense.

After 15 minutes' play, torrential rain added to the mix making even simple passes more difficult. Quality passing football? None to be seen. Steve Edwards, attending his first live Albion match, stood damply on the Woodman Corner, next to a Villa lover. The Villa man's comment on anything and everything was: "Stone the crows!"

Against the run of play, Gerry Hitchens scored for Villa in the 65th minute. "Stone the crows!" The linesman had raised his flag for offside but referee Rosekilly gave the goal anyway without consulting him, to the undiluted fury from the soggy Baggie crew. Did Villa *always* have such luck?

But news quickly reached the Hawthorns via the old wooden scoreboard that Manchester City were 3-1 up against Leicester and with an extra 15 minutes to play too. With the bizarre nature of goal average calculations, a further goal for City meant the big drop for Villa unless they scored a second themselves.

The Aston mob's dilemma of whether to stick or twist was solved for them by waves of attacks from the home side. They were damn lucky to be a goal to the good, and scoring a second was impossible given their back foot position. Albion pressed forward relentlessly. Despite the exquisite passing skills of Ray Barlow, the guile of Ronnie Allen and the power of the Tank (Derek Kevan), bloody Villa continued to hang on. Thus far, the evening was proving to be a horrible re-run of the FA Cup semi-final but with added rain. That Villa's unsegregated supporters looked as though they'd had teeth extracted without anaesthetic was feeble consolation. At Maine Road, Man City were still seeking a killer fourth goal.

The Villa manager Joe Mercer left the ground early, in a splendid early example of Villa arrogance. Apparently a banquet in aid of Billy Wright was considered more important than guiding his team to safety. Mercer was in for fearful indigestion later.

There were just two minutes remaining when Ronnie Allen changed history. Supporters at the Smethwick End had a clear view as the little maestro pounced on a loose ball on the edge of the penalty area. As if in slow motion, he pivoted on the spot, losing his marker in the process. ALLEN swivelled and struck the ball perfectly. Robin Hood couldn't have shot a straighter arrow. The shot had 'Goal' written all over it and before keeper Sims could move, the ball was in the net. Albion players swamped Ronnie in a welter of sodden blue and white striped shirts. The Villains sagged. "Stone the crows!" was the Woodman Corner wail.

Ronnie Allen later claimed to friends that he'd mishit the shot and he didn't actually want to score. "I didn't really mean to score. I just swung my foot and it flew into the net. I did feel bad in a way." He was in a very small blue and white minority along with the club directors. More positively, Ronnie acknowledged he had never heard Albion supporters cheer as loudly as they did at that moment.

Such was the noise level that few actually heard the final whistle. Albion had relegated Villa. Savour those words. Albion relegated Villa. Word quickly reached Maine Road of Allen's landmark achievement. Manchester City stuck with their three goals, content to play out time to remain in Division One. Stone the crows indeed.

By then both sets of supporters had left the Hawthorns, walked to the bus stop and boarded buses after much patient queuing. The rival fans chatted politely amongst each other as if it had simply been another 'run of the mill' game. But it was anything but that.

v Plymouth Argyle 5-1
FAC3. Att: 21,901
5 January 1963

Albion	Plymouth Argyle	Referee
Potter	Maclaren	R. Smith
Howe	Reeves	
Williams	Fulton	
Cram	Williams J	
Jones	Fincham	
Drury	Newman	
Jackson	Lill	
Fenton	McAnearney	
Smith	Jackson	
Kevan	O'Neill	
Clark	Maloy	

THE WINTER of 1963 remains infamous to this day. In the current global warming era, it's hard to imagine weather so inclement and so prolonged that the Baggies were unable to play competitive football for two months. Prior to the Cup match at Plymouth, Albion's previous three League matches were all postponed. Every minor road in Birmingham and the Black Country was virtually impassable but employees were still expected to get to their workplace, so they walked, or rather slithered, regardless of the distance. An unofficial work-to-rule at power stations didn't exactly help either.

But there was hope for Plymouth. Devon was the only part of the country relatively clear of snow, aided by salt resident in the top layer of soil. But on the previous Tuesday, snow fell heavily in Devon, 'the worst for 82 years.' Parts of the county were buried under 24-foot drifts. One newspaper reported on the plight of 14 marooned guests at the Forest Inn. The only item that licensee Mr Bridges had in quantity was whisky. How would they manage?

Plymouth Argyle, fourth in the Second Division and unbeaten at home all season fancied their chances against such glamorous opposition. They badly wanted the game on because of the incentive of an above-average gate. Volunteers struggled to clear the pitch of snow and subsequently keep the turf ice-free. They were succeeding until an additional four inches of snow descended on the Friday. A local referee inspected the pitch and would not commit himself beyond agreeing to a further inspection on Saturday morning. With no choice but to travel, the Albion team caught the train south. "All that was missing was the club sledges. We had everything else," said a club spokesman. The train journey took seven hours, two hours longer than normal.

Argyle summoned a tractor to clear the pitch once more. A team of volunteers worked late into the night under floodlights to clear the snow from the terraces and move it to a safe location. The match referee made a late night inspection and declared that the cup tie was 99 per cent likely to be on, but further inspections would be necessary on Saturday morning.

That decision was too late for Albion supporters. Over 600 had bought seat tickets and nearly all anticipated travelling by train on a football special. But British Rail cancelled the train late on Friday with many supporters already at the station. Some raged, others wept. A few more determined supporters pondered alternatives. The well known Harold Whitehouse from Stone Cross managed to travel overnight by rail on an excursion ticket. He was to spend the whole of Friday night travelling to Devon.

Meanwhile, Ken Goode, treasurer of the Oldbury Branch of the WBASC, had organised two coaches to leave the Black Country at midnight with an assortment of spades and shovels in the boot. Just reaching the departure point was a challenge for most. "When we left," said Ken, "somebody said 'I don't know if you are good supporters or plain nuts'. Perhaps it's a mixture of both." The trip was an act of faith with no motorway network, only limited knowledge of road conditions and coaches with few driver safety aids. The two vehicles were quickly separated in the dark. Despite the best efforts of the drivers, the coaches repeatedly slid off the road. But the Baggie contingent would not be defeated. Tired, working in the dark and armed with only a few shovels and determination, they got their transport back on the road and kept going. Their persistence got its reward. The first coach struggled into Plymouth at 9 o'clock with its shattered passengers. Its twin needed a further hour, ten in all, to complete the trip.

The second coach arrived just in time for the third pitch inspection. The verdict was worrying. The referee discovered patches of ice on the pitch and was concerned about players' safety. Yet another inspection was scheduled. Cursing, the weary volunteers worked on – scattering sand over the pitch and raking the remaining snow. Meanwhile the equally weary supporters joined the players on Plymouth Hoe. A newspaper photographer captured a group of fans without hats and gloves, wearing only light coats – perhaps 'plain nuts' *was* the more accurate description.

Such single-mindedness deserved reward and they duly got it at 1pm when referee Smith pronounced the game on – one of only five in the country to proceed. Now all that was required was the players to show their appreciation by winning the game.

Albion were in supreme form and this continued when BOBBY CRAM provided them with an early lead, receiving a neat pass from Fenton. Argyle fought back, striking the Albion bar and then equalising through McANEARNEY. Yet they could not match the Baggies' skill levels and they were done for when centre-forward Alec Jackson was carried off with a broken leg, following an accidental clash with Graham Williams. With only ten men, Plymouth were quickly undone by KEVAN's header. Later goals from SMITH, NEWMAN (og) and a close range shot from KEVAN in the 89th minute completed a thrashing. The home side never found an answer to Derek Kevan's power, the speed of Clive Clark and above all the class of new boy Ronnie Fenton in the Albion attack. Manager Archie Macauley was pleased: "I am well satisfied with the result."

The gallant 200 supporters (augmented by sailors who originated from the Midlands) felt rewarded for their efforts. Harold Whitehouse, who faced his second successive night on a train, said: "The lads played really well. It's a good performance to win 5-1 away from home at any time, though I was a bit disappointed in Plymouth's display." Friends of Harold knew that was as enthusiastic as he ever got.

The gallant 200 also had bragging rights: 'I got to Home Park', or even, 'I saw Albion score this year.' The Baggies managed to put on a home game against Sheffield Wednesday the following Saturday (losing 3-0) but would not play again until March.

v West Ham Utd 4-1
League Cup Final, 2nd Leg. Att: 31,925
23 March 1966

Albion	West Ham Utd	Referee
Potter	Standen	(Unknown)
Cram	Burnett	
Fairfax	Peters	
Fraser	Bovington	
Campbell	Brown	
G. Williams	Moore	
Brown	Brabook	
Astle	Boyce	
Kaye	Byrne	
Hope	Hurst	
Clark	Sissons	

ALBION AGREED to enter the League Cup for the first time in 1966. And what a splendid fist they made of making progress in the competition. Walsall, Leeds, Coventry, Villa and Peterborough collectively conceded 23 goals as the Baggies reached a two-legged final against West Ham. The first leg was in London and mercifully, Jeff Astle was fit after a full three months' absence. The King marked his return with a goal but a Johnny Byrne strike in injury time gave West Ham a slim 2-1 advantage. The margin seemed very narrow against such an attack minded side as the Baggies. Johnny Kaye, who eventually amassed 23 goals that term, finished only as Albion's third highest scorer.

Over 32,000 assembled at the Hawthorns. Their number included Ernie Hunt, who owned a café near Villa Park despite his Albion support. He was not going to let a small matter of a knee operation stop him getting to the Hawthorns, so Ernie got out his crutches and struggled through the turnstiles. Not only did Ernie and his fellow fans have the King to admire again but also inspirational Albion midfielder Bobby Hope, following his absence for a full month. The Baggies really wanted the Cup as Tony Brown explains: "We were so keen to get out and play that night that the lads were banging the dressing room door." Or as Skipper Graham Williams puts it: "You can have no real idea of how badly we wanted to win. Not only for ourselves, but for the club … for the town … and for the supporters from all parts of the Midlands."

The Albion men could almost inhale the polish on the Cup. They hit the Hammers hard. Johnny Kaye came close twice in the opening minutes as the visitors wilted under the onslaught. Their defence half cleared Bobby Hope's lob but allowing the ball to reach Clive Clark was not a great idea. Chipper, in one sweet movement, set up JOHN KAYE to score from 18 yards. The Hammers' aggregate lead had lasted just nine minutes. In truth, they were lucky to preserve it for that long. The Hawthorns crowd, led by a frothing Brummie Road End maintained a terrific roar, demanding Albion attack even more.

Charge forward they did. Johnny Kaye latched onto a Jeff Astle pass on the edge of the area but could only hit a Smethwick End spectator rather than the net. Such was Albion's dominance that a second goal wasn't long in coming. It went to TONY BROWN, bravely getting his head amongst a crowd of defenders to put away Cram's lob. Despite playing on the wing, it was the Bomber's tenth goal in the League Cup that season including at least one in every round.

West Ham were unsure in defence and lacked their opponents' attacking drive. Bobby Moore spent the first 30 minutes in midfield, making a minimum contribution. Martin Peters was bizarrely playing at left-back and Geoff Hurst was marked out of the game. It was the less heralded John Kaye who was the star man with his high workrate and menacing of the opposition defence.

Albion had completely turned the game around and there were still 72 minutes to go. They could have relaxed, sat on their lead, but that is not the Albion way. After all, hadn't their manager Hagan told them over and over again: "Above all, our first duty is to entertain the public and go for goals."?

With the Hawthorns crowd bellowing "Hagan, Hagan" in homage to their manager, CLIVE CLARK's diving header made the score 3-0 on the night. This after just 26 minutes! The Londoners continued to look more and more wobbly under the goals avalanche. Their forwards weren't receiving any possession to work with and so the ball kept coming back into their own goalmouth.

Bobby Hope started a flowing move through Albion's midfield. Cue more dazed, confused defenders leaving space for the unlikely GRAHAM

WILLIAMS to blast home the ball from 25 yards via two bounces and in off a post. It was the left-back's first goal for over a year. Normally only a *Roy of the Rovers* team goes 4-0 up in the first half of a Cup final.

Only with the game out of their reach did the visitors press forward with any menace. It must be said that their impetus was more to do with WBA easing off rather than their own prowess. Albion remained comfortable. Brabook hitting the post was the closest West Ham could manage.

There were only fifteen minutes remaining when MARTIN PETERS managed a no-consolation when he finished off a Sissons centre. It was too late to make a difference. As Graham Williams had it: "Only an earthquake can stop us now." No-one on the terraces was stressing too much, more just counting down the minutes until their new Cup holder status could be confirmed. Albion still had opportunities as time ran out. West Ham keeper Standen certainly earned his wages that night.

This was Albion's night and Albion's Cup. Wrote journalist Tom Duckworth on the devastating first half: 'Albion played the finest football I have seen from them since their ten men won 5-1 at Forest in 1958.'

In their entire club history, the Baggies have only secured two trophies on their own pitch. With a 46-year gap since Championship silverware was previously presented in 1920, this was a marvellously enjoyable night for the Baggie hordes pouring onto the pitch in triumph.

Graham Williams led his Cup-winning team into the Directors' box to receive the trophy and their individual silver tankards from Football League President Len Shipman. For every member of the team, this was the biggest honour they'd ever won. Albion had also qualified for the Inter-Cities Fairs Cup for the first time ever – a chance to do battle against mysterious football clubs…foreigners!

v West Ham Utd 4-0

League Cup semi-final, 1st Leg
Att: 30,193. 18 January 1967

Albion	West Ham Utd	Referee
Sheppard	Standen	J.A. Cattlin (Rochdale)
Cram	Burnett	
Williams	Burkett	
Collard	Bovington	
Jones	Brown	
Fraser	Moore	
Brown	Brabook	
Astle	Peters	
Kaye	Byrne	
Hope	Hurst	
Clark	Sissons	

ALTHOUGH THE Baggies were League Cup holders and thus playing in Europe for the first time, 1966/67 proved something of a trial. Goals were conceded far too regularly with only one clean sheet before Christmas and the team never quite gelled as a unit in the first half of the season. With 14 defeats in their first 21 games, relegation became a serious worry. And yet in the League Cup they'd not lost a game in their two seasons of entry. Albion started their defence of the trophy with their now customary thrashing of the neighbours. The 6-1 demolition of Aston Villa was followed by defeats of Manchester City, Swindon and North-ampton (only just relegated from the top division) in quick time with fifteen goals scored with the opposition only collectively amassing four. Their semi-final opponents were West Ham. The Hammers were favourites for the trophy according to the bookies and had all three of their World Cup winners in Moore, Hurst and Peters to call upon. The bookies noted that in a League game just a few weeks earlier, West Ham won comfortably 3-0 – part of a worrying sequence of only one win in the last eight matches for the Black Country club.

But Albion had the King – Jeff Astle. The King rather liked playing West Ham and Bobby Moore in particular. He'd already found the net in five different matches against the Hammers and his appeal in East London mirrored that of say a Bull, Stein or an Adebola to later generations of Albion supporters. Tony Brown summed up: "Jeff always liked playing West Ham. None of their defenders could head a ball."

This year, the first half of the two legged affair was at the Hawthorns. With some of the latecomers still shuffling onto the terraces, the Baggies found the net in the first minute. Inevitably, it was ASTLE who did the damage, out-jumping defender Ken Brown as they battled to reach an Ian Collard cross. Whatever grandiose plans the London side had around keeping the game tight and scoreless went out of the window at that point.

The vast majority of the 30,000 crowd roared their approval. The visitors had barely recovered their composure before the Baggies fatally hit them again. The West Ham goalkeeper Standen bellowed furiously at his defenders about lack of protection as top scorer CLARK had ample time to finish off Kaye's low cross.

Both Clark and Kaye were playing with a rare freedom, almost as if they'd just been released from prison. Their opposition was edgy, ragged and looked uncomfortable. John Kaye charged through a wide open rearguard and shot at goal. The ball rebounded via a defender to ASTLE who was in the right place at the right time to score again. The Baggies were 3-0 up in the first half. History doesn't record where the much vaunted Bobby Moore was positioned but it clearly wasn't goalside of the King. "Ass-tul, Ass-tul," chorused the Brummie Road in homage of their goalscorer.

The contrast between the two teams was immense. West Ham's defence was all over the shop. Heads were down and morale was even lower. Meanwhile, Albion, sensing blood continued to charge at their dazed opposition. Astle, seeking a hat-trick, put one effort just wide and then had a 'goal' chalked off, for allegedy being offside though he vehemently denied committing any offence. The King would not remain frustrated for long however and just before the interval, ASTLE confidently steamed past two men and defeated Standen from ten yards to complete a marvellous hat-trick.

The half-time score was exactly the same as in the League Cup final Second Leg the previous year. Had West Ham learnt nothing about Albion? That and no doubt many other home truths were pointedly made by the management to their hammered Hammers.

The break permitted the Londoners to get their heads together and it was a wholly more determined West Ham who attacked their Midland counterparts in the second half. The Baggies were obliged to use their third choice keeper Rick Sheppard due to ineligibility and injury. The hapless Sheppard had only returned from honeymoon the previous day. He could have sat in a deckchair licking an ice cream during the first 45 minutes but now he was called upon as the Hammers battered his goal. The young Bristolian was in fine form, stopping shot after shot. He even remained unperturbed when Geoff Hurst fell on him – which appeared to be the World Cup winner's major contribution. Journalist Gron Williams noted 'that neither a shot nor header went past him, not a dangerous cross escaped him as he dashed out bravely to intercept.'

With the second half being end to end, Albion also had their moments. Just one fingertip denied Clark Albion's fifth goal and then the referee disqualified an Astle goal for the second time. Didn't the man know real talent when he saw it? West Ham's increasingly desperate efforts brought no practical reward; Bevington striking Albion's crossbar was the nearest they came all night. As the Londoners could not penetrate Albion's defence, 4-0 presented an impossible score to retrieve. Deep down Albion knew they were Wembley-bound though in public they tried to play down their elation. Captain John Kaye was understandably delighted by the score: "What a wonderful feeling. It was like coming out of a dark tunnel to realise at last we had hit our top form."

In the second leg three weeks later, West Ham went all out on attack for goals. They managed two but Albion took advantage of their opponents' necessarily scant defence to find the net twice themselves through Hope and Clark. WBA won 6-2 on aggregate and at that moment believed they were on the way to retaining their Cup. We'll draw a hasty veil over events at the first Wembley League Cup final .

v Liverpool 2-1

FAC6 – 2nd replay. Att: 56,139
18 April 1968

Albion	Liverpool	Referee
Osborne	Lawrence	(Unknown)
Clarke*	Lawler	
Williams	Hughes	
Fraser	Smith	
Talbut	Yeats	
Kaye	Strong	
Brown	Callaghan	
Collard	Hunt	
Astle	Hateley	
Hope	St John	
Clark	Thompson	
Sub: Stephens*	Sub: Wall	

IN THE mid-1960s Liverpool were formidable: League Champions in 1964, FA Cup Winners in 1965 and League Champions again in 1966. As the 1967/68 season reached its zenith, they were just one win behind the League leaders. The Reds could score goals but with names like Hughes, Smith, Lawler and Lawrence in their defensive ranks they were even more adept at stopping them – by fair means or foul.

When the Cup draw paired Albion with Liverpool in the quarter-final, the Midlanders were written off – the Reds had already beaten them twice in the League. Yet the Baggies were hardly cannon fodder. They were in eighth place in the top flight and although they were too inconsistent to threaten the leaders they were physically strong and boasted two supreme goalscorers in Jeff Astle and Bomber Brown. Furthermore, following a fortunate escape in Round Three at Colchester the Albion men genuinely believed their name 'was on the Cup'.

Conventional wisdom had it that the all-conquering Reds would draw 0-0 at the Hawthorns (which they did) and win the replay at Anfield (which they didn't thanks to the intervention of King Jeff). All experts confounded, the Black Country's finest or 'sacrificial goats' as one press hack had it, squared up for a third time against the Red Machine.

An evening encounter at Maine Road was hardly an equitable distance between the two clubs in those pre-M6 days. Yet around 17,000 Albion-ites headed north for an evening kick-off with the mass outbreak of buried grandmothers and life-threatening flu that had kept them off work remark-ably behind them. The midweek travelling number was mightily impres-sive yet the Baggie ranks were outnumbered more than two to one by the Reds. Liverpool fans were everywhere, notably surrounding the Albion coach as they travelled along the East Lancs Road from their break in Southport. As Tony Brown recalled: "It was horrendous, we were getting dog's abuse from these fans, they were all signalling it was going to be 2-0 or something! Actually, it wound us up a bit, it probably helped."

The noise level was ear-splittingly high, completely drowning out the best efforts of the Greater Manchester Police Band. The Baggies' followers were determined not to be outdone and after all they literally had hope – their midfield revolved around Bobby Hope and having been forced out of the first two matches by injury, he was finally fit to do battle at Maine Road.

The Black Country side took an unexpected lead in the 7th minute. Collard caught Smith and Callaghan with an 'after you Claude' moment with neither intercepting his through ball to Astle. 'Flying Pig' Lawrence came out of his goal but ASTLE beat him, drilling the ball low and hard just inside the right hand post. The Brummie Road, temporarily housed in the Kippax, celebrated wildly. For the first time in the marathon tie, Liverpool had fallen behind.

Uncharacteristically, the Baggies fell back into defence and quickly surrendered midfield superiority. Worse, big John Kaye was struggling at the back following a painful clash of heads with his own team-mate John Talbut. After ten agonising minutes on the sidelines, he returned with a thin white headband covering his badly gashed forehead. He was later to receive ten stitches in the wound.

Even though John Osborne performed magnificently, the ever advancing red tide was too much. Six minutes prior to the interval, TONY HATELEY headed an equaliser following a left wing cross from Callaghan.

Liverpool were out for the kill but Albion continued to remain resilient. Doug Fraser, swearing horribly, and Graham Williams were defensive Trojans. 'Ossie' Osborne in goal was simply magnificent, denying the bulldozing body of Ron Yeats and making a full length diving save from Roger Hunt. Then, gradually, the Baggies fought back, pushing away the Liverpool stranglehold.

The Hope, Stephens and Brown midfield trio combined together on the right flank to produce a smooth series of passing movements that were a delight on the eye. Substitute Kenny Stephens played Astle in, the King found Tony Brown who touched the ball on and there was CLARK on hand to jab the deciding goal just inside the far post, despite a lunging heavy tackle. The Kippax erupted. So did the Liverpool defence who vainly claimed for offside.

The Scousers had less than half an hour to save themselves. Their goose could have been completely cooked had Kenny Stephens's effort not been disallowed for offside several minutes later. But Liverpool survived and their combined desperation and physical strength forced the Baggies back onto the defensive.

The pressure seemed incessant. John Osborne later described the last few minutes as "the Charge of the Light Brigade" as wave after wave of red shirts sought the elusive equaliser regardless of cost. Huge defender Ron Yeats battered Albion's keeper to the ground in an attempt to reach one cross; Ossie had a new injury to complain about.

Just when mass heart attacks seemed inevitable, the final whistle sounded. Some Albion supporters wept with relief. The Baggies were in the last four of the Cup for the first time in a decade.

As the weary, sweaty faithful filed out of the ground, a thunderstorm of almost apocalyptic proportions rent the night sky. It was almost as if the Gods wished to pay tribute to the Albion performance.

Soggy Black Country train travellers headed for Manchester Piccadilly. They filed onto the Birmingham platform only to discover that directly opposite were equally wet hordes of red shirted Liverpool supporters miserably queuing for the train to transport them the short distance back to Lime Street. The Baggie crew mentally prepared for an abusive exchange or worse but were taken aback by shouts of, "Well done Baggies – now make sure you beat that lot from the other end of Stanley Park!"

v Manchester United 6-3

Att: 45,992

29 April 1968

Albion	Manchester United	Referee
Osborne	Stepney	H. Davey (Dorset)
D. Clarke	Dunne	
Williams	Burns	
Brown	Crerand	
Talbut	Sadler	
Fraser	Stiles	
Rees*	Best	
Collard	Law	
Astle	Charlton	
Hope	Kidd	
Hartford	Aston	
Sub: Lovett*	Sub: Foulkes	

ALBION WERE FA Cup finalists; Manchester United were League Champions, League leaders and en route for a European Cup final. It was small wonder that this Monday night fixture was such a major draw.

Baggies follower Rick Janowski, then 14 years old, recalls: "Evening games for me always provided an extra 'something' in terms of atmosphere. It was noisy and exciting with larger than life colours of the teams against a backdrop of grass that was almost fluorescent under the floodlights. United were top of the league, but the Baggies were having a very good season. For all of the stars that United brought with them (Charlton, Best, Law…), the Albion team of that era didn't feel second best to anyone, not even the team that was destined that season to be the first English club to win the European Cup. So a win seemed a perfectly reasonable expectation, which added to the excited anticipation of the fans."

But so many fans! The official gate of 46,000 crammed into the Hawthorns; thousands more were locked outside. This was danger level cramming particularly after a gate was broken down, allowing even more supporters free access into the ground. One local photographer captured the moment as an injured woman was placed on a stretcher, suffering from a crush injury from a swaying crowd. In the background the picture indicates with post-Hillsborough hindsight just how tightly packed the Hawthorns audience was. Fortunately most small children were sat safely in rows on the running track. There was a fatality that night as a man died from a heart attack. It isn't clear whether the gentleman would have suffered the attack regardless of his surroundings. What remains quite shocking even then was the corpse lay on a stretcher under a blanket at the Smethwick End behind the goal because the emergency services had no way of removing him from the ground.

The future kings of Europe launched themselves immediately at the Albion rearguard with John Osborne needing to be at his best to keep out Denis Law and Brian Kidd. The first goal seemed only minutes away. Indeed it was but unexpectedly it was JEFF ASTLE who scored it. He intercepted a wretched and indecisive backpass from Dunne, dodged past Law and blasted the ball into the top corner of the net.

Dunne's error was to be typical of a wretched night for the United defence or as journalist Colin Malam put it: 'an unbelievably pathetic thing of rags and tatters'. Alex Stepney in the United goal made save after save from the rampant Baggies. Nobby Stiles was so irritated by his team's shortcomings that he bravely (or stupidly!) brawled with Jeff Astle, who was at least a foot taller.

Stepney couldn't hope to keep out the Baggies by himself and sure enough he was beaten again, this time by RONNIE REES finishing off an impressive surge by Bobby Hope. United defender Francis Burns had an opportunity to clear but took too long and Albion's Welsh winger nipped in. According to supporter Rick Janowski: "Bobby Hope had a superb game. He produced inch-perfect cross-field passes that left United defenders sliding and scrambling. Every time the pass slipped straight to the feet of oncoming Albion forwards."

The benefit of a Matt Busby team talk at the interval spurred on the Reds and they attacked with renewed vigour. But their back door was still jammed open. The still fuming Nobby Stiles crudely brought down Ronnie Rees in the penalty area and BOMBER BROWN scored from the spot. Such was the ferocity of the tackle leading to the penalty that Rees was immediately substituted. Law came closest to a goal for the visitors with John Osborne tipping his shot over at the second attempt. 3-0 and still 35 minutes remained.

Three minutes later a Bobby Hope free kick was perfectly weighted for ASTLE to head Albion's fourth. Despite the galling defeat, United fans continued to sing and chant for their team and they finally received a long overdue reward. Doug Fraser conceded a penalty and DENIS LAW marginally improved the score to 4-1. Law nearly scored his second but Ossie was equal to the task with a splendid reflex save.

Naturally in this topsy turvy and incredibly open game, back came the Baggies and scored again. For once, King Jeff didn't make proper contact with his head from Tony Brown's centre but no matter because ASA HARTFORD was on hand behind him to score. The teenager was thrilled with his first ever goal in what was only his second first-team game.

Journalist Colin Malam again: "Albion's ability to sweep through the United back division almost at will drove their normally sedate supporters into a wild frenzy of excitement and exultation." There was yet more to celebrate as ASTLE completed his hat-trick with a diving header at the far post. This was the fifth threesome of his career. "Astle for England!" was the passionate cry. The King now had 31 goals to his name (and famously went on to score another hat-trick just two days later against his favourite whipping boys West Ham).

Naturally with a 6-1 lead, Albion could afford to ease off, even against frantic opposition who could see their title slipping away. BRIAN KIDD restored some balance to the scoreline with two late goals in the 77th and 81st minutes and Denis Law missed several openings to narrow the gap further. Yet it was Albion's night after a quite magnificent display. At the end of the game, Albion supporters charged onto the pitch from all directions to salute their team (or to escape the crush?).

United's loss of two points plus the indignity of their heaviest defeat for five years went a long way to handing the League title to rivals Manchester City. Just two matches later, their big city rivals secured the Championship… by two points. Albion? They had the small matter of the Cup final to look forward to.

v Everton 1-0
FA Cup Final. Att: 100,000
18 May 1968

Albion	Everton	Referee
Osborne	West	L. Callagham
Fraser	Wright	(Merthyr Tydfil)
Williams	Wilson	
Brown	Kendall	
Talbot	Labone	
Kaye*	Harvey	
Lovett	Husband	
Collard	Ball	
Astle	Royle	
Hope	Hurst	
Clark	Morrissey	
Sub: Clarke*		

I N THE 1960s, the FA Cup final was the only match guaranteed to be shown on live TV across the country. For many people, it was their sole opportunity to watch a top side in action for the full 90 minutes. It was football's showpiece occasion. Anybody who was anybody had to be there, with even a few tickets put to one side for the silly sods who actually supported the two teams. Albion received 18,000, way below their average attendance. Rail travel remained popular in those pre-motorway network days. Eight special trains were offered by British Rail; 'New multiple units, holding 900 people!' the advert read excitedly. As for the remainder, with car owners still very much in the minority, local coach firms found themselves having to scour the entire area for sufficient borrowed charabancs to augment their own fleets for the day.

On paper, Everton were the stronger side, and proved it two months earlier by completing a double with an embarrassing 6-2 victory at the Hawthorns. Skipper Graham Williams confidently pronounced: "No team beats another three times in a season." Everton weren't WBA's only worry. Following Albion's dismal League Cup final result the previous year, reaching the twin towers again was tinged with fear of failure and a second successive Wembley defeat. "All I could think of," said Jeff Astle, "when we got in the dressing room, was our hammering by Queen's Park Rangers."

For the outsider, the 1968 Cup final was a turgid game, low in skills, involving players who seemed to prefer kicking each other to actually kicking the ball. Supporters who remember the 60s Albion team through rose-tinted spectacles forget how sponge men (hardly physios: usually hardbitten ex-pros given to wielding the 'magic sponge' in a threatening manner whenever injured, prostrate players threatened to disturb their matchday peace and tranquility) were required by 11 different players in the first 30 minutes. Doug Fraser needed three stitches in his knee; John Kaye had an injured foot (and famously became the first man to be substituted at Wembley). Both dressing rooms, post-match, must have resembled a First World War dressing-station.

But Albion were as much sinning as sinned against; a surprisingly lenient referee simply compounded the problem. Even normally wall-eyed, partisan supporters showed their mutual frustration by chanting: "We want football!"

Jeff Astle was left isolated up front. Regular lifeline Clive Clark was unusually subdued on the wing. Unable to make any headway against the towering Labone, Astle regularly drifted wide in search of possession, but rarely found much. Talk about the irresistible force meeting the immovable object; with John Talbut similarly the master of Joe Royle at the other end, mutual frustration was pretty much guaranteed.

The Everton midfield trio of Ball, Harvey and Kendall ('the holy trinity') did fashion a couple of openings that Osborne was equal to. Once he was beaten by Royle's head, but John Kaye was crucially placed on the line to clear. The pattern continued with Albion threatening, occasionally, but it was mainly Everton creating and – crucially for the Toffees' fortunes that day – missing.

Then, with only five minutes remaining, the Scousers thought they'd won the Cup. Morrissey's lob into the danger area found Husband completely unmarked, but with only Osborne to beat, he somehow blasted right over the bar. So, with both lots of followers wearily resigned to yet another dose of torment, the match dragged itself into extra-time.

It was while both sides, now grouped into weary, sweaty huddles, were receiving hasty tactical instructions from their respective gaffers that the weather decided to impose its belated presence upon the proceedings. For almost the entire duration of the preceding 90 minutes, the clime had been a pretty accurate reflection of affairs upon the pitch: damp, dull, and drizzly. But as both sides took their respective places for extra-time, all that was to change dramatically. Suddenly, those slate-grey clouds acquired mobility, dramatically parting, to afford a single, broad, golden shaft of late May sunshine admittance to the bit of Wembley pitch where stood the Baggies: for sheer Biblical drama, even Cecil B. deMille couldn't have orchestrated it better.

Said nerve-frazzled teenager Glynis Harrison, to her equally-fraught uncle, standing alongside: "Blimey, 'the sun shines on the righteous'?"

Too right. No sooner had the words left her lips, a certain Mister ASTLE embarked upon the goalwards run that would assure him an eternal place in Albion's already impressive Cup history. As King Jeff himself explained: "I had a crack at goal, but it wasn't a very good shot. I had a bit of luck with the ball bouncing back to me, but this time I could see the whole goal, and hit it on the volley with my gammy left foot. To me, though, it was just as if God had said on Friday night 'The final will end 1-0, and Jeff Astle will score the goal.' My name was on it."

Every Baggie just knew where that ball was heading – and when it did, the entire Albion end went absolutely crazy. Glynis's uncle had more reason than most for doing so. Having 'invested' heavily at the bookies when the Baggies were about 50-1 to lift the pot, he now stood to collect about a thousand quid, courtesy of the King! Given that the average working man's wage was about £20 per week back then – not bad!

There was more drama near the end when Albion's Lovett almost made it two, after a solo run virtually the length of the pitch – only to see his lung-busting effort land in Row Z. Everton piling on the last-minute pressure, Ossie belting every high ball in sight with his fists, total adrenalin overload imminent… but then it was all over. Realisation dawned: we'd done it, the proof there for all to see when Graham Williams held the precious pot, now thoroughly sun-sparkled, aloft from the Royal Box.

v Carlisle United 4-1

League Cup semi final, 2nd Leg Att: 32,791. 3 December 1969

Albion	Carlisle United	Referee
Osborne	Ross	(Unknown)
Fraser	Hemstead	
Wilson	Caldwell	
Brown	Passmoor	
Talbut*	Winstanley	
Kaye	Ternent*	
Krzywicki	Brown	
Suggett	Barton	
Astle	Hatton	
Hartford	Balderstone	
Hope	McVitie	
Sub: **Martin***	Sub: **Murray***	

ON THIS damp, freezing night, the Baggies had a problem. If they were going to reach Wembley for the third time in four years, they had to retrieve a one goal deficit from the first leg against their defensive Second Division opponents plus their 4,000 noisy followers.

Albion's manager Alan Ashman knew he was in for an awkward night. As a former United manager, the club was special to him: "I didn't really want us to face Carlisle in the semi-final but it was always going to happen. I watched them beat Oxford in the quarter-final and felt ill at the thought of coming up against them, not because I feared them but because I knew it would be emotional for me. At Carlisle, they should have beaten us by three or four goals. I told my players afterwards, 'You lot have got out of jail here, take the initiative and let's beat them at our place.'" United won 1-0 but with Ossie Osborne having a grim night, which would literally give him nightmares for weeks, the visitors considered themselves fortunate.

The Baggies had the additional pressure of supporters' expectations at a well-attended but not full Hawthorns. As a decent top flight side, hosting lower Division opposition should not be a problem. On paper.

Predictably Albion attacked while Carlisle sat back. For all their first half possession, the Baggies were not making any progress against the deep defending Cumbrians, who chased, ran and harried their big name opponents. The Baggies forced a series of corners but were unable to force the ball over the line.

An injury to defender John Talbut forced a re-shuffle into a bold 3-3-4 formation. United took advantage of the additional space and counter-attacked. Bob Hatton even struck the upright in the first half and Carlisle's Brown missed a fine chance after Ray Wilson lost the ball in his own penalty area. A couple of inches were all that separated the Baggies from a very difficult position indeed.

The ever near-paranoid Ossie was having a rotten night. "I have never been so nervous over a game of football in my life. I was scared of making a mistake as another Carlisle goal could have finished us. I was so on edge that even when I was taking goal kicks I kept thinking *well if I give this to one of their players and let the side down ...* Talbut going off made it worse."

There was no score at half-time and not much to enthuse over. John Kaye admitted later to "being rather worried". Bobby Hope was convinced "it was one of those nights". Veteran supporter Steve Carr, then aged just eight retains only one memory from this match: "I felt so wretchedly nervous during half-time." Gloom spread quickly. As the second half began, the dread in the air was now palpable, reminiscent of a Hitchcock film with the tension ratcheted up with each passing minute. Think Southampton, May 2008 without a second match safety net. Reporting for the *Birmingham Evening Mail*, Dennis Shaw commented, 'for much of the game, there was an atmosphere of near silence.'

The Cumbrians continued to enjoy the key moments. Bob Hatton collected the ball in the first minute after the break, beat off Yorky Kaye's challenge and struck the ball past Ossie in the Albion goal. The ball hit the far post and bounced out to the edge of the penalty box. Barton was perfectly positioned to score but he panicked and missed. There were anguished howls of frustration from the Brummie Road (and from the away end!). This was not in the script.

Yet increasingly there were signs that the Cumbrians were feeling the pressure. Instead of passing the ball out of defence, they were increasingly resorting to aimless hoofs.

Then came the turning point. United keeper Ross beat Astle to Fraser's cross but his clearance dropped beautifully for BOBBY HOPE. The midfielder controlled the ball and made space for a shot. Hope hit the ball perfectly through a tangle of legs into the net. The wild and unrestrained celebrations that followed were primarily from relief. Carlisle were undone. Yet Ossie's worries continued: "Instead of getting over my nerves, I started to worry then about Carlisle breaking away and me making a mistake."

Albion's forwards lusted for more, urged on by a now raucous home crowd. Ten minutes later, Ray Wilson made a superb crossfield pass to Bobby Hope. Sir Bobby played in COLIN SUGGETT at the far post to tap in the second. And there was more to come – four minutes later the keeper was penalised for taking too many steps. Bobby Hope rolled the ball gently to BROWN and … thump … goal! That thump could be heard all around the ground.

The shell-shocked visitors tried to rally but the game was up and they knew it. Colin Suggett lobbed an opponent cleverly before setting up DENNIS MARTIN to drive past Ross for their fourth goal in only nineteen minutes. Curiously, some Albion supporters made for the exits.

Four minutes from time, FRANK BARTON finally found the net for United but it was too little, too late. Albion would be travelling to Wembley three months later for the third time in four years. The post-match celebrations were surprisingly low-key with only a handful of youngsters running onto the pitch. Older, wiser heads were still reeling from relief.

Long term supporter 'Stroller' enjoyed himself: "It was the best night I remembered in the Brummie. The singing, the joy, the celebrations and the surges down the terraces. You could move 20 or 30 feet in one of those surges. We'll never see the likes of that again."

Alan Ashman couldn't win personally whatever the outcome. "We only just beat them," he admitted afterwards." The final score didn't tell the true story." Neither did he. An unnamed Albion player confessed, "There's a bit of colour back in the gaffer's face. He was ****** white at half-time."

v Oldham Athletic 1-0
Att: 22,356
24 April 1976

Albion	Oldham Athletic	Referee
Osborne	Ogden	Ray Tinkler
Mulligan	Wood	
Cantello	Whittle	
T. Brown	Bell	
Wile	Edwards	
Robertson	Hicks	
Martin	Blair	
A. Brown	Shaw	
Mayo	Robbins	
Giles	Chapman*	
Johnston	Groves	
Sub: Robson	Sub: Brannigan*	

UNDER THE guiding hands and feet of new player-manager Johnny Giles, the Baggies perfected a compelling style of possession football. They didn't score many goals but they conceded far fewer and were very hard to beat. As a consequence, the team were able to string together an impressive series of results. The Hawthorns faithful could feel proud to be Baggies after the miserable, depressing Don Howe era. Reaching the 1970 League Cup final seemed a long time ago.

Bolton Wanderers, holding the last promotion spot (no play-offs in the 1970s) looked increasingly anxious as the Black Country's finest reeled them in match by match including a 2-0 victory over Wanderers at the Hawthorns. Bolton's nailed on promotion was slipping away due to their series of unexpected defeats. And then Albion were past them as the finishing straight hove into view. Holding their nerve, the Baggies had a one victory lead with just two fixtures remaining. In the first of the pair, Albion could only manage a 0-0 draw against Leyton Orient at Brisbane Road, though were ultimately grateful for the point as Orient spurned decent chances to win. Their advantage had been cut in half so the scenario became brutally simple. Albion had to beat struggling Oldham Athletic at Boundary Park to win promotion back to the top flight. It sounded straightforward yet the Latics had only lost two home matches all season and would secure a wage bonus if they could finish in the top half of the table. In addition, they'd actually scored more goals than Albion.

Naturally this was a game not to be missed. Some 120 coaches were mustered from across the conurbation and beyond which were all filled in Cup final style. Many others chose to drive the relatively short distance to 'Ice Station Zebra' as Oldham's ground was frequently called due to its exposed nature. "Everyone's Albion mad," remarked Secretary Gordon Dimbleby as the Club Shop remained under siege for much of the week.

The residents around Boundary Park probably expressed similar feelings as 12,000 Black Country folk descended upon them. The club commissionaire was heard to exclaim "Christ, you've brought the whole bloody town with you." The road network couldn't cope as Tony Brown remembers: "There were so many Albion fans going to the game we couldn't get off the motorway and had to have a Police escort to Boundary Park. In the dressing room before the game everyone was incredibly nervous, and then I'll always remember walking on the pitch and seeing a mass of blue and white. It just hit you. All the players looked at each other as if to say, 'We've got to do it for them today'."

Inevitably, this League match felt more like a cup tie. Play was frenetic and the noise constant. Len Cantello did little to endear himself to the outnumbered Oldham crowd when his tackle on Les Chapman led to the midfielder being carried off after 19 minutes. No beach holiday for you next week…

Albion needed time to get their possession football going, time which almost cost them when David Shaw nearly beat Osborne; thankfully Ossie was equal to the task. Still, the visitors did eventually make some progress, stringing together a fine move from which Bomber Brown narrowly missed his target. Space was hard to find as marking became tighter and tackling became fiercer. Many anxious glances were cast at the ever incendiary Willie Johnston. This was not the day for him to lose his head. As half-time approached, Joe Mayo headed just wide of Ogden's left hand post. Cue agonised expressions all round.

With news filtering quickly around the ground that rivals Bolton Wanderers were winning their match, the second half became even more tense. Tempers frayed on the terraces as Oldham continued to be stubborn party poopers. This was not in the script.

Then in the 55th minute 'IT' happened. Paddy Mulligan fed Mick Martin down the right wing. Martin returned the ball to Mulligan and his cross was nodded down by Ally Brown for BOMBER BROWN to blast the ball through a crowd of players with his left foot. Most of the stadium erupted and headed for the pitch. When order was restored, "and now you're gonna believe us…the stripes are going up" was bellowed to the rooftops.

Brown almost scored a second but the rest of the 90 minutes was a tension-wracked exercise in possession football and craven time wasting. John Wile recalls: "We kept getting time signals from the bench and mentally I tried to tick off the seconds." In the closing minutes, John Osborne prevented a change in the course of history with a full length hearts-in-mouths save.

Referee Ray Tinkler used his instrument as an inadvertent party starter. Once again the jubilant Albion support poured onto the pitch – this time to celebrate promotion.

Champagne corks were popped on and off the pitch. Burly Black Country blokes were spotted in tears and all because of what Oldham born Tony Brown had achieved for that day for his club and for the supporters on that beautiful spring day. Johnny Giles and his team made an appearance in the main stand to huge acclaim. It was a scene that supporters were reluctant to leave.

Yet more extraordinary scenes followed on the way home, with the team bus royally escorted all the way down the M6 by a phalanx of supporters' coaches. With no restrictions in that era, alcohol flowed freely on board every vehicle. In some ways, the happy procession resembled a Black Country re-make of *The Italian Job* sans cliff. Holding court on the team coach was an obviously well oiled Willie Johnston, giving the royal wave to all and sundry, wearing the most devilish ear splitting grin as he did it.

Promotion was a new, heady experience for Albion supporters. WBA were previously promoted in 1949 and until three years previously, the issue of needing to think about promotion had not arisen. The Baggies were back where they belonged.

22 v Manchester United 3-2
FAC4 replay. Att: 37,792
1 February 1978

Albion	Manchester United	Referee
Godden	Roche	George Courtney
Mulligan	Nicholl	(Spennymoor)
Statham	Albiston*	
T Brown	McIlroy	
Wile*	Houston	
Robson	Buchan	
Martin	Coppell	
A Brown	Jordan	
Regis	Pearson	
Trewick	Macari	
Johnston	Hill	
Sub: Hughes*	Sub: J Greenhoff*	

"I HAVE NEVER been involved in anything like these two games against United. There was so much drama and atmosphere that anyone who saw them will remember them for a lifetime." – Ron Atkinson.

There almost wasn't a match at the Hawthorns to remember. The Baggies had taken on the Cup-holders at Old Trafford and deservedly took the lead through Willie Johnston. Despite the vocal excesses of an unusually loud Stretford End, the classy visitors didn't look in any trouble. But calamity struck in the last minute as Coppell equalised via the back of Godden's head. Willie Johnston claimed to be unperturbed: "We'll murder them in the replay – they were lucky today."

Albion's recently appointed manager Ron Atkinson probably couldn't believe his good fortune to take over at a club which didn't need a major rebuild. He was so new to the Baggies that the replay was his first home match in charge.

An all-ticket 38,000 crowd at the Hawthorns turned up, hoping to see exactly that. Regular Albionites could justify sipping milk, while smugly pronouncing (without the Scouse accents) *"Manchester United – who are dey?"* United had not won at the Hawthorns for 12 years and had been trounced 4-0 on both their previous visits, the most recent being only 5 months earlier. However, the Baggies were under-strength with Cunningham unfit and Robertson suspended, which was a potentially serious problem for such a small squad.

The weather was simply vile, near monsoon standard. Yet the mud, high winds and rain actually enhanced the spectacle by adding doubt to otherwise predictable play. It was the home side who scored first. A Willie Johnston cross was knocked down by Ally Brown into the path of his namesake TONY BROWN who struck the ball sweetly into the net while still on the run. There wasn't too much time for the Brummie Road to bask in the reflected glory or taunt the self-important Mancs that they were handing over the FA Cup as the visitors equalised nine minutes later. Future Albion coach STUART PEARSON finished off a four-man move and the Reds were back in business.

Albion remained on top with midfield pairing Mick Martin and John Trewick in superb form, seemingly everywhere at once. On the wing, Willie Johnston was at his mercurial best – a single defender was never enough with United regularly needing to double mark him. In theory this left space elsewhere providing Willie could remember he did have team-mates...

Mainly thanks to first class blocks from both keepers, there was no more score until after the restart. Willie again did the damage, flighting in a splendid cross from the left wing which struck the bar; CYRILLE REGIS reacted quickest for an easy tap-in.

Prospects were looking rosy for the Baggies but then Joe Jordan and John Wile clashed in a heading duel. Wile went down immediately, blood spurting from a broken cheekbone. The pair had a history of disputes and most onlookers were convinced that hate figure Jordan led with his elbow. The stricken defender explained: "I knew when I went down that something was broken. I know what happened and so did he but I'm not talking about it. Let's just say that his elbow and my face collided." Albion now had a problem with both regular central defenders out of action. Substitute Wayne Hughes, a distant relative of Emlyn, was only 19 and was yet to start a game.

Ron Atkinson instructed the youngster to fill in for Wile at the back. As soon as he was on the pitch, Paddy Mulligan overruled the new manager. He remembered Martin playing in central defence for his country and so told Martin to play at the back and young Hughes in midfield.

Revenge and counter revenge was sought as the match deteriorated. United had bigger, harder players but that didn't stop Willie Johnston from taking out McIlroy. On another night, he would have walked. Even with an unlikely central defensive partnership of Robson and Martin, the Baggies continued to hold out with supporters excitedly hailing a brilliant victory. United had other ideas. With only 15 seconds to the end of the match, GORDON HILL smashed a spectacular goal… off Godden's head again. United's doggedness to retain their trophy had forced extra-time.

Such a crushing setback would have finished many teams. Neutrals would be happy for 30 minutes more of this spectacular affair but neutrals weren't at this game. To concede so late was horribly, horribly flattening. Most of the Hawthorns was silent as the teams readied themselves for extra-time.

Albion needed something very positive to take the strain off their temporary defence. Remarkably, within one minute they got it. Big CYRILLE REGIS did the damage, crashing the ball home via the crossbar. It was a magical moment, coming so soon after the deflating equaliser. The joyful roar was probably audible in West Bromwich town centre. In their excitement, supporters in the front row of the normally sedate Rainbow Stand were spotting capering on the perimeter wall and even on the roof of the executive boxes.

United wearily slogged forward through the mud and driving rain in search of a third equaliser. They were to be denied at every turn. Albion's midfield did their best to shield their makeshift defence while behind them the defenders were unfazed by the increasingly desperate Greenhoff, Jordan, Pearson and Co, despite their superior physical strength. Minutes had to be counted down but they went past without any serious alarms. Cup-holders Manchester United were beaten by the Baggies… again. Such was the exciting nature of the spectacular mud-spattered battle that the seated supporters rose to offer all the players a standing ovation.

Both local and even national press were fulsome in their praise for this vibrant occasion. Ray Matts from the *Birmingham Mail* wrote: 'This was soccer in all its glory. Not a sport strangled by safety first tactics but a full blooded passionate confrontation for success rather than survival.'

v **Nottingham Forest** 2-0

FAC6. Att: 36,506
11 March 1978

Albion	Nottingham Forest	Referee
Godden	Shilton	B.Partridge (Cockfield)
Mulligan	Bowyer	
Statham	Clark	
T.Brown	McGovern	
Wile	Needham	
Robertson	Burns	
Martin	O'Neill	
A.Brown	Gemmill	
Regis	Withe	
Trewick	Woodcock	
Johnson	Robertson	
Sub: Cunningham	Sub: Johnston	

THIS YEAR, 1978, was the year of the Clough. Having just escaped the clutches of the Second Division the previous season, he'd added modestly to his promotion squad, splashing out big money only for the England international goalkeeper Peter Shilton, who'd had enough of Stoke. The result was a team where the end product was far greater than its component parts. Forest set about winning all the domestic honours by leaning heavily on their impressive defence. When March rolled around, the East Midlands outfit were in the League Cup final and were clear League leaders in addition to the small matter of an FA quarter-final tie against WBA. Horrifically from an Albion perspective, Nottingham Forest were unbeaten in 42 League games. They were simply the best club in the country. Their wisdom of recording a song with the lyrics, 'the best team in the land' was questionable as it would surely wind the opposition up.

The quarter-final caught everyone's eye. All tickets were sold very quickly in these pre-live match days. Such was the interest that Lenny Henry was to feature a sketch in his comedy programme around his attempts to get into the Cup match without a ticket.

Derek Statham bravely declared: "I'll bet Forest are as much concerned about us as we are them." There was some justification in his observations for the Baggies were a decent top drawer side themselves. In the FA Cup, they'd famously knocked out the holders Manchester United and beaten another top division side in Derby County on their own pitch. Any Albion side where Laurie Cunningham was only on the bench must have been pretty damn good.

As the players took the field, it was clear that Willie Johnston was in playful mood. He was wearing a tartan hat, his way of making a point about his Scottishness to Archie Gemmill. Unlike some of his predecessors, new manager Ron Atkinson (this was his fifth match in charge) was completely at ease with such flamboyance.

Ultra-confident Forest did all the early pressing. At the back, the old stagers Wile and Robertson marshalled their troops for a long siege. But despite their best efforts, Forest continued to make inroads and Tony Godden had to make two magnificent saves. A goal wasn't far away…but it was Albion who scored it. MICK MARTIN spotted Shilton off his line and delicately lobbed him. At the time it seemed no more than a very happy fluke from a very occasional goalscorer, but TV replays were to indicate the goal was no freak. As John Wile said later: "It was a far more skilful and well intended goal than a lot of people thought at the time." It was Martin's last ever Albion goal.

Intentional or not, the Baggies now had an unexpected lead to defend. Even better, with neither of Forest's workaholic midfielders McGovern and Gemmill appearing to be fully fit, Tucka Trewick and Mick Martin had far more of the play than they imagined. Gemmill had an altercation with fellow Scot Willie Johnston and was booked, which limited his activities even further.

Albion were moving the ball around confidently with Willie Johnston in exuberant mood. Famously, he managed to trap the ball with his bottom, a trick he'd attempted several times but was rarely able to master. The Hawthorns collectively roared appreciation and as Willie noted: "Brian Clough was up off the bench going berserk, and once we'd wound him up, we felt we were on our way." Forest had more possession but Albion had more of a cutting edge. Ally Brown had a glorious chance to double the lead when he pounced on a Kenny Burns error but could only toe-poke the ball the wrong side of the post.

With his side trailing, Clough's team talk probably blistered the dressing room walls. Yet all his profound bluster and his players' hardened resolve came to naught because within 60 seconds of the second half the Baggies had doubled their advantage. There was no real sophistication about the move. Paddy Mulligan launched the ball long behind the Forest back-line, CYRILLE REGIS was quickest to react and with the Reds' defence still turning, he had time to thump a low shot past Shilton. That second goal was vital. At the time, Willie Johnston was thinking, almost praying, 'For God's sake, don't miss that you big sod.' Fortunately Cyrille didn't miss and the big striker deserved every one of the repeated emphatic chants of "Cee-rul!" It was his sixth goal in the FA Cup that season, yet he hadn't scored in the League since October.

Forest looked dazed and confused. Defeat was unthinkable but coming back from 2-0 down looked equally unlikely. Yet slowly they did force their way back into the ascendancy, urged on by their pride or their fear of Clough. Perhaps both. Robertson was a menace on the wing, so too was Woodcock's mobility and horribly hairy Withe's power in the air. Albion were hanging on, supporters nervous. Surely a semi-final place couldn't slip away now? Woodcock found too much space before any defender could react. He shot … inches over the bar. Again Forest attacked and this time it was the hirsute Peter Withe who lost his marker. His header was on target but Godden made a one-handed save. Time was against Clough's men and their efforts became increasingly frantic against a stubborn defence until there was no time left at all. Partridge's last blast on his whistle was sweet music to Albion and their supporters. They'd beaten Forest – a feat no-one else in the country could manage. West Bromwich Albion and their new media-friendly manager made back page headlines.

Cup-holders knocked out, League leaders despatched the same way. Who could possibly stop Albion winning the Cup now? The semi-final draw against struggling Ipswich only strengthened the belief that this was going to be our year…

v Manchester United 5-3
Att: 45,091
30 December 1978

Albion	Manchester United	Referee
Godden	Bailey	G.F. Owen (Anglesey)
Batson	B.Greenhoff	
Statham	Houston	
T.Brown	McIlroy	
Wile	McQueen	
Robertson	Buchan	
Robson	Coppell	
A.Brown	J.Greenhoff*	
Regis	Ritchie	
Cantello	McCreery	
Cunningham	Thomas	
	Sub: Sloan*	

THE 1978/79 season included so many delights that supporters of limited means could afford to pick and choose without feeling as if they were missing out. By Christmas, Albion had already recorded six away League victories and had also reached the UEFA Cup quarter-final. The immediate post-Christmas period consisted of back to back away matches at the famous Arsenal (which became away win no. 7) and mid-table Manchester United.

"Not Old Trafford again," wearily tutted the regulars. Although the Baggies hadn't tasted victory in Salford for 16 years, they'd drawn their last three visits. United needed to be wary of the Stars in Stripes, not the other way around.

Thus the turnout of the Black Country's finest supporters in the high cage-like pens that constituted the away accommodation was described at best as modest. There wasn't much enthusiasm elsewhere either with a comparatively meagre attendance of 45,091. The Cup match between the two sides ten months earlier had attracted an additional 12,000 supporters. The weather was certainly a factor, with vicious sub-zero temperatures frankly painful on the skin. The pitch was solid and would be considered unplayable a decade later.

Taking the pitch was the best Albion side in the last half century – strong, determined and quick with a manager who let his players make their own decisions. They boasted eight wins and two draws in their last ten matches and the overhyped Salford crew were in their sights.

However it was United who made the first impact. After Wile and McIlroy became entangled, the referee unhelpfully awarded a drop ball just yards from the goal. A scramble ensued with Brian Greenhoff attempting to lob Godden. 'T.G.' tipped the ball over, but the danger was not over. From the resulting corner, Ally Brown attempted to clear but that man GREENHOFF was in the way and he volleyed the ball power-fully past the startled Godden.

A goal down at Old Trafford? No problem. United's lead lasted just six minutes. Len Cantello wide on the right played a neat ball inside to BOMBER BROWN and the former United fan guided a low shot just inside the post. Jumping up and down in the away pens relieved the onset of frostbite a little. We were still celebrating the first goal as the second went in. Regis and Cunningham bamboozled the home defence with Regis setting up LEN CANTELLO with an astute backheel and the City fan found the roof of the net. Later he said, "I wish I'd had a Man City shirt on under my Albion one. I'd have whipped the West Brom shirt off straightaway. "

Albion followers were celebrating taking the lead when suddenly it was gone. The giant McQUEEN rose to meet and direct a free kick perfectly. Three goals in three minutes – rare stuff indeed.

Four whole minutes later it was the Reds' turn to lead. SAMMY McILROY twisted and teased his way into the penalty area and defeated Godden from 12 yards. Five goals in thirty minutes – what was next? Another Albion surge of course! Robson's shot was goalbound until Bailey tipped it around the post. Ron Atkinson had seen enough and headed for the dressing room.

Derek Statham takes up the story: "We came in at the break buzzing after Bomber had knocked in Len Cantello's cross right on half-time to make it level. But the ground was different then, the manager didn't walk down the touchline to get to the dressing rooms, they went through the stadium somehow. So we got in the dressing room, Big Ron was waiting there for us. 'You're playing brilliant lads, don't worry about the score, keep playing that way and you'll get the equaliser.'

He'd missed the goal because he'd set off for the dressing room just before the whistle. So we're looking at each other and then somebody said, 'Boss we just scored, we're level.' 'Are we? Brilliant!' Ron replied, 'Just keep playing and you'll get the winner!' That was typical Ron, just gave us so much opportunity to play the way it came, play naturally."

And Albion did keep playing, much to the chagrin of United keeper Gary Bailey. As the England international ran towards his goal to resume the match, he mimed with his fingers and a puzzled expression to show he'd lost count of the score. It was a brilliant cameo.

Bailey was quickly in action, attempting to stop 'Pop' Robson from adding to the score. To his relief, McQueen hacked the ball off the line. Robson claimed vainly that the ball had crossed it. The one way traffic continued with Bailey repeatedly denying Regis. One save was outstanding with the goalkeeper's body parallel to the crossbar but barely a foot below it to preserve his goal. United, bar one piledriver from Ritchie, were hanging on against the yellow and green tide. It was a football feast, albeit one which couldn't keep the savage cold out.

Then, with 16 minutes remaining, Godden's long clearance was astutely headed on by Regis to CUNNINGHAM who outpaced the United defence and tucked a low shot into the corner of the net. "Oh … what a goal!" screamed commentator Gerald Sinstadt over one of the most regularly viewed Albion goals ever. Indeed it was an extraordinary goal, though the commentator did lose credibility when he regularly confused the lean Cunningham with the broad Regis.

United had nothing more to offer. Ally Brown somehow scooped Batson's centre over the bar from only feet out just a couple of minutes later. Still the Baggies charged forward and fittingly it was REGIS who settled the match with just five minutes to go, set up by the unselfish Ally Brown. Although the away victory was saluted by the frozen few, it was the fifth away win in a row and almost taken for granted. The magnitude of the performance only sunk in later when everyone had thawed out – a pity because three decades later we still await another win at Old Trafford.

v Aston Villa 1-0
League Cup Quarter-Final. Att: 35,197
20 January 1982

Albion	Aston Villa	Referee
Grew	Rimmer	Ray Chadwick
Batson	Swain	
Statham	Gibson	
Brown	Evans	
Wile	Williams	
Robertson	Mortimer	
Jol	Bremner	
King	Shaw	
Regis	Withe	
Owen	Cowans	
Mackenzie	Morley	
Sub: Bennett	Sub: **Bullivant**	

RONNIE ALLEN'S Baggies side was a strange mixture, a post-Robson apocalypse. The defence was sound with the classic Batman, Del Statham, Ally Rob and Johnny Wile quartet still in place. The midfield included classy performers like Gary Owen and Steve Mackenzie. Yet the engine room lacked pace and width and were dependent on the excitable Martin Jol for tackling. Up front was basically Cyrille plus one. The League season was a long frustrating slog but in the cups the Baggies were determined, gritty and highly successful.

December was a fine month for Albion. They won all four of their League and Cup matches and Ronnie Allen won Manager of the Month. Baggies lover Amanda Miles recalled: "From the moment I heard the cup draw driving along the Coventry ring road, I was counting the days until the game. We were invincible around then and so felt highly confident as we took on the true and only enemy of the time – the hated Villa. Another glorious moment of self-actualisation in Maslow's Hierarchy of Needs!"

Amanda's observations were those of a fan of a confident team (only one defeat in the previous fourteen games – inevitably to bloody Stoke), curiously unfazed about playing the League Champions (and sadly imminent European Cup Winners' Cup) on their own pitch.

The winter of 1981/82 was vicious and subsequently the fixture fell victim to a couple of postponements. Villa had 400 tons of snow to shift before the two sides could finally do battle in front of a 35,000 attendance. Visiting Villa Park felt more discomforting than normal. Only 7 months earlier, we'd doggedly frustrated the Championship-chasing home side for 85 minutes, and were in a great position to divert the trophy to Ipswich instead. Then a weak backpass by Brendan Batson was pounced upon by werewolf-lookalike Withe. The away following that night has still to come to terms with this awful error decades later. So has Batson!

For the big Cup match, Albion were unashamedly defensive, relying on their solid back four to keep the home side at bay. They relied on the galloping Statham using his pace to set up a chance for big Cyrille. Protecting their back four was Martin Jol, 'a massive and confident lynchpin' according to *Birmingham Evening Mail* journalist Leon Hickman. Villa found a determined and aggressive Albion thoroughly difficult to break down. Only the pace of Morley and Gibson plus the fumbling by keeper 'Barney' Grew gave the visitors any concerns.

The Baggies created only a single chance in the first 45 minutes... but what a chance! Villa's Evans headed a Statham cross out to Gary Owen. The Mancunian made for the touchline before picking out STATHAM at the far post. In a moment of poetry, the full back headed the ball beyond the grasp of Rimmer. Statham didn't score many but each one had significance. This one felt very special. We'd have kissed him if we could have got close enough.

Frustration mounted quickly for the Seals of Aston. League Champions are not supposed to lose to old rivals at home. They'd already had one appeal for handball turned down against Jol early in the game and when two more followed, also against the tall Dutchman, their fury overflowed. The vehement protests by Morley to a linesman were noted by the referee who dismissed him during half-time for foul and abusive language. This was Morley's first ever dismissal. "I get kicked up in the air every weekend and never complain. What kind of justice is there when I am sent off for a few swear words?" he moaned later.

There was genuine puzzlement when the home side re-took the field with only ten men. Crammed in the low fenced terrace behind one goal, Albion supporters didn't know why Morley had gone and happily chorused, "Where's your Morley gone?" Scowling Villa supporters seemed to be gesturing their side would score twice but in reality without Morley, scoring just one was a big ask. Albion remained cautious, sticking firmly to their 4-4-2 formation. With defender Evans marking Regis ('he found him about as generous with space as a broiler farmer' according to Leon Hickman), the visitors didn't have much attacking impetus anyway. Only once did Cyrille break free when in the 58th minute, he shot just over the crossbar.

Easily mastering his defensive duties, Derek Statham regularly rampaged down the left wing. England manager Ron Greenwood was an interested spectator and afterwards he admitted, "I was impressed with [Statham's] composure and skill on the ball and his goal crowned a very good performance." He was both full back and winger in an otherwise narrow formation.

Villa continued to huff and puff, trying to ignore ever louder songs from Albion supporters enquiring about their missing winger and reminding them of the score. Mark Grew had to tip over a top corner-bound effort from Gary Shaw in the 74th minute. This was as close as the home side were ever to come to an equaliser. Albion carefully ran down the clock and then celebrated gleefully with supporters at the final whistle.

Amanda Miles recalls: "My mum and I were seated among Villa fans in the Trinity Road stand but had to declare ourselves as Statham scored that glorious headed goal. At the final whistle the miserable Villa fan next to me said with typical Villa generosity in defeat, 'You'll lose to Spurs in the semi-final.' I agreed with him to keep him happy but I couldn't have cared less – we were in the semi-final of another cup competition having won in the arch enemy's camp. Was there anything better? Sadly there have been few more memorable moments since that day in my watching of the Baggies."

Moments of triumph have to be fully celebrated there and then because one never knows when the opportunity may re-occur. Over a quarter of a century later and we're still waiting for a repeat Villa Park victory.

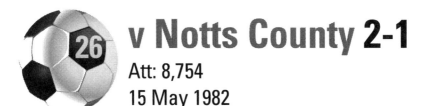

v **Notts County** 2-1
Att: 8,754
15 May 1982

Albion	Notts County	Referee
Godden	Avramovic	John Deakin
Batson	Benjamin	
Statham	Lahtinen	
Bennett	Goodwin	
Wile	Kilcline	
Webb	Richards	
Mackenzie	Chiedozie	
Cowdrill	Hunt	
Regis	McCulloch	
Owen	Christie	
Monaghan	Mair	
Sub: Cross	Sub: McParland	

THE PRICE Albion's unbalanced side paid for their runs to both cup semi-finals was a terrible run of form in the League. The Baggies lost six League matches in a row immediately after the painful defeat by QPR in the FA Cup semi-final. Albion appeared to have turned the corner with a brutally fought 2-1 victory at Wolverhampton which virtually relegated the home side and ought to have made Albion safe. Maddeningly, three more consecutive defeats again left WBA in serious danger of losing their top flight status. They had just three matches remaining and the second and third of these were against the equally desperate Leeds United...and bloody Stoke. To stay up, Albion had to win two of the three. The first match, at Meadow Lane against mid-table Notts County was vital.

Albion had only one goalscorer in Cyrille Regis. Despite painfully limited support, he'd finished 23 chances prior to kick-off. Elsewhere, central defender Martyn Bennett filled in as a midfield destroyer, Webb made a rare appearance in central defence in his stead while left-back Cowdrill played left midfield. This was a patched up side, low on confidence, but they still had senior players like Batson, Wile, Owen, Godden and Statham in their ranks.

Three days earlier, the team had a heart-to-heart as Tony Godden explained: "Everyone had to forget that perhaps they had a friend sitting next to them and say, openly, what they felt. Some of the younger players did not seem to realise what could happen to us. They believed that being too good to go down was enough and it was left to the more experienced players to say what was in front of us."

Notts was an easy trip for the faithful to make – particularly on a baking hot day. The lack of a roof on County's awkwardly shaped and rather flat terraces behind a floodlight was, for once, rather welcome. The Magpies were notoriously badly supported in their ramshackle ground with the attendance under 9,000. Not that Albion's gates were significantly higher at the time – disillusionment with negative, frightened football, fear of violence and many other factors had home attendances around the 12-13,000 mark. But when times are hard, you find out who your real friends are. Despite feeling punch drunk and fearing the worst, over 2,000 shirt-sleeved Baggies determinedly did their best to aid the cause.

Our bellowed encouragement unexpectedly paid off very early with STEVE MACKENZIE beating County keeper Avranovic with a low shot from 20 yards after David Hunt had felled Regis. With only five goals to our name in the past eight matches, this huge bonus was gratefully seized upon.

Albion defended their lead in a surprisingly robust manner. It was alien to our nature yet as long as our goal stayed intact, no-one from WBA was complaining. That goal represented confidence, a talisman that must be defended. The few home supporters were howling in protest as Albion bodies went in hard. Even Owen, who normally couldn't tackle his way out of a paper bag, had caught the 'they shall not pass' mood. Every minute which passed was gratefully acknowledged. County however were becoming increasingly persistent with Mair and Hunt testing Tony Godden. The half-time interval allowed breath to be released.

It was the visitors who then took the ascendancy. There was little chance of Albion adding to the score but at least the home side seemed to have lost interest in the heat. Still the tackles were flying in from Albion with Owen, Bennett and Wile all duly noted in notebooks. The delicate Owen chopping down Pedro Richards was particularly suprising – what was in their pre-match drinks?

Then...horror. Completely against the run of play, CHIEDOZIE headed an equaliser. Albion reeled drunkenly. A draw would leave them next to bottom and given the need for six points from nine, one point was of no real value.

Sickened supporters stretching for a clear view around the floodlight tower tried to rally the troops. Albion tried to come again, snapping into tackles and looking for a way forward. "We set out with the firm intention of coming out of every 50-50 situation with the ball," John Wile declared later. But the home side were threatening to overwhelm them.

Our prayers were answered. REGIS ran onto a through ball from Steve Mackenzie, came out best from a 50-50 tackle outside the penalty area with keeper Avramovic and calmly slotted the ball into the net. The joy was barely describable. Big Cyrille vanished under a heap of players while supporters hugged sweaty strangers. "It was the most important one I'd scored all season," Regis admitted after the game.

If Albion were determined before, they were even more so now to retain their lead. Everybody behind the ball, blocking, tackling, kicking...simply horrible to watch. With more belief in our voices, there was a new spark in the chants of "We are staying up...we are staying up."

The match moved into injury time, the amount of which was then only known to the referee. Gary Owen lunged at McParland with both feet and was sent off. Such incidents involving Owen occurred as rarely as an eclipse of the sun, but this was no time for discussing records. Now down to ten men, we felt more vulnerable and defended even more deeply, fearing the unknown quantity of added minutes. The referee was watched constantly and as soon as that familiar gesture was made, we were punching the air. The relief was immense after so many defeats.

The three points kept us out of the bottom three and laid a firm foundation for survival. Notts fans were unhappy with both the match and the visitors, chanting "animals" at the celebrating Albion players. But sometimes needs must. As John Wile explained: "We did what was necessary to win. In our position, you don't expect pretty football." Belief restored, beating Leeds United 2-0 just days later completed the job.

v Millwall 5-1

League Cup 2nd Round, 2nd Leg.
Att 13,311. 25 October 1983

Albion	Millwall	Referee
Barron	Wells	J.Hunting (Leicester)
Whitehead	Lovell	
Cowdrill	Stride	
Zondervan	White	
McNaught	Nutton	
Bennett	Cusack	
Lewis	Robinson*	
Thompson	Lowndes	
Regis	Bremner	
Owen*	Neal	
Perry	Chatterton	
Sub: Cross*	Sub: Martin*	

TALK ABOUT being up against it – the task was to recover a 3-0 first leg deficit albeit against a team two divisions lower. The match at the Den was simply 'one of those nights'. Albion, 7th in the top flight, were shorn of many of their big names through injury. Within five minutes they were two goals in arrears and in great difficulties. The Baggies were forced into playing two 18-year-olds in central midfield and by the end had an unlikely looking central defensive partnership of Clive Whitehead (full back or winger) and nineteen-year-old John Smith playing his one and only first-team match. During the 90 minutes, Albion's black players were routinely racially abused while the whole side had to endure spitting and coins hurled by the East Enders. On three occasions the home crowd invaded the pitch. Arguably, the Albion supporters had an even worse night with a coach being stoned and turned around before kick-off.

Today Premier League players would just shrug and forget the League Cup but back then, maddened by their treatment the pride of the Black Country wanted revenge. Manager Ron Wylie, a man not really given to saying much at all opined: "I have never seen the players in such a determined mood." Derek Statham added: "I've put a bet on Albion going through." The Baggies' cause was aided by the return of defender Martyn

Bennett, a genuine leader who never missed an opportunity to explain how much he disliked Cockneys. After his first leg substitution, lumbering but effective central defender McNaught had recovered to play alongside Benno. Classy midfielder Gary Owen was also fit.

When the two teams took to the field they found it partly occupied by Millwall supporters. All night, their large and malevolent presence acted as both an incentive to Baggies supporters and players alike and a disincentive to fans who had kept away. The attendance was only 13,000, a poor turnout for the time and 4,000 of that number were from the East End. Late afternoon, lurid stories of Millwall elements rampaging around Birmingham New Street station deterred the undecided.

Kick-off was delayed while the pitch was cleared of unwelcome visitors. Albion's initial surge was met by flying boots from the London team and missiles from behind the goal. Big Garry Thompson was put clear but the Millwall keeper smothered the chance, accompanied by repulsive ape noises. The whole evening was becoming thoroughly distasteful. The visitors kept nine men behind the ball at all times and tried to harry the top Division team out of their stride, by fair means or foul. Three visitors were booked in the first half. The Baggies were struggling for space and all too often reduced to using Stoke City tactics, hammering high balls in the direction of big strikers Thompson and Regis. The pair were simply crowded out.

The primary concern for the Hawthorns regulars was wondering where and when the next group of Millwall hooligans would reveal themselves. They'd already seen Londoners taking over part of the Rainbow Stand. Compared to their safety, providing vocal support for their own side was a poor second.

With only five minutes before the interval, the Baggies made a key breakthrough. An intuitive run and pass from Owen found GARRY THOMPSON unmarked in the penalty area; with opponents appealing vainly for offside, Thommo hooked the ball into the net.

Now there was hope and fresh belief. Albion were showing their class. Mickey 'Fatty' Lewis was winning every tackle in midfield and overlapping full back Clive Whitehead was an easy outlet ball because of his pace and know-how; Garry Owen's left foot waved like a wand. Up front, Regis and Thompson were like rampant bulldozers with teeth clamped and foreheads furrowed against the insults. There was new belief on the hitherto nervous Brummie Road. "Come on you Baggies," had a new tingle in every voice.

However there was a danger that the interval could disrupt the flow of the home side. Instead, the Baggie Boys re-took the field with even more belief and within three minutes REGIS thundered the ball under Wells following a short corner from the right.

Millwall were ragged and crumbling under the pressure. Cusack lunged wildly at Thompson and conceded a penalty. OWEN slotted the spot-kick perfectly, right inside the post for the equaliser. Cue cheering, stamping, leaping Albion supporters while Police again literally wrestled for control of the away end.

When Owen picked out THOMPSON for a bullet header past the thoroughly dejected Wells for Albion's fourth, this provided the cue for a favourite old song. It was both predictable and pleasurable. "Millwall, Millwall, what's the score?" A pointed jibe delivered with rare vehement exuberance.

And still Albion weren't done. The Londoners hung on desperately but there was no stopping CYRILLE REGIS who hit his shot so hard into the top corner it almost burst the net. 5-3 on aggregate. Take that.

The Baggies were content to play out time. However, there was a slight scare in the 93rd minute when Millwall's DAVID MARTIN scored from a corner. But it was far too late to make any difference against an Albion side so rampant they could have taken on the world. It was our night and rarely did victory taste so sweet.

There was an immediate price to pay as the maddened seated section of the away support reacted aggressively. They ran over the top of the corrugated executive boxes in the Rainbow Stand to get to their tormentors in the Brummie Road. The outnumbered Police just about managed to keep the two sides separate.

Laughably, post-match the Lions manager George Graham complained about his team being intimidated, saying: "I am thankful we finished with 11 players left on the field. Albion softened us up and then went for the kill. I have players with gashes across their noses caused by elbows." Ron Wylie summed up the club reaction perfectly: "It's just sour grapes."

Beating Stoke 3-2 to win a first ever trophy, the Staffordshire Cup, in 1883 is ample reason to celebrate the club's first ever picture.

Albion's 1888 FA Cup Final side. Preston's so-called Invincibles were defeated 2-1.

With the 1892 FA Cup Final making it four appearances in only seven years in England's glamour tie, West Bromwich Albion were one of the country's most famous clubs. Villa were flattened 3-0.

One goal was enough to beat the Terriers as WBA became 1911 Division Two champions.

In 1911, Sid Bowser scored one of the goals in a 2-1 win before the Lincoln hooligan firm took over.

A moment to savour for the 1920 League Champions. Chelsea were thrashed 4-0.

Just one of WG 'Ginger' Richardson's brace in the 1931 Cup Final which Albion won 2-1. Just days later another WG strike helped the Black Country's finest to promotion.

Not satisfied with winning the Cup in 1931, this XI were aiming to get into Division One in the same season ... and they made it – just, thanks to a sweaty 3-2 victory against Charlton.

After several years of near misses, the rebuilt 1948/49 team returned WBA back to the top flight with a cracking 3-0 win at Filbert Street.

Walking out at Wembley for the 1954 FA Cup Final against Preston North End.

"Running round Wembley with the Cup". The Preston tormentors celebrate after their 3-2 triumph.

Bobby Robson scoring one of his team's five goals in an extraordinary FA Cup replay at Nottingham Forest in 1958.

... But the win at Forest was in vain as the Baggies lost 1-0 at a rabid post-Munich Old Trafford.

During the infamous 1963 mid-winter Manager Archie Macauley discusses the finer points of snowploughs prior to a cracking 5-1 win at tractor-cleared Home Park.

Tea or coffee, chaps? The 1966 League Cup winning get down to serious celebrations.

They shall not pass. The Baggies stubbornly defend their 4-0 lead in the 1967 League Cup semi-final, once again against the Hammers.

The King with the Cup. Jeff Astle's solitary extra-time goal delivered the trophy to the Black Country in 1968.

"Of course it's milk!" Ray Wilson and Doug Fraser celebrate reaching the 1970 League Cup Final following a hard-fought 4-1 victory over Carlisle.

THAT day at Boundary Park. 'Bomber' Brown's goal in April 1976 sends Albion back up.

At a hot Meadow Lane in 1982, Steve Mackenzie goes for goal. A 2-1 away win was essential to keep WBA in the First Division.

A Cyrille special and the living is easy. Nottingham Forest are going out 2-0 in the 1978 FA Cup quarter-final.

Tony Morley competing against the fish lovers. The visitors were in for a nasty shock in the last few minutes in 1984 as their 1-0 lead became a 3-1 defeat ... such a shame!

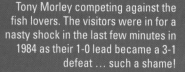

"Reidy, he's trying to eat our trophy."   "I know… Just keep smiling." Humbling Port Vale 3-0 at Wembley '93 – does it get much better?

Kevin Donovan makes some Dingles very cross by netting during their 3-2 defeat in September 1993.

Lee Ashcroft used his head at Fratton Park in 1994 for the only goal. A rare experience.

What a feeling! Richard Sneekes gets that swamped feeling as Megson's men retain their second tier status in 2000 thanks to two late goals against Charlton.

He's in there somewhere! Igor Balis savours his very late winner in April 2002 meaning promotion was only one game away.

The ultimate goal. SuperBob clinches a first ever promotion to the Premier League with the second goal in a 2-0 defeat of Palace in 2002.

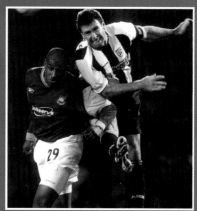

Gregan gets his, er, big frame in the way. A 3-0 deficit at Upton Park in November 2003 amazingly became a 3-4 away win.

The great escape! A 2-0 defeat of Pompey in 2005 saw the Baggies safe for another Premier League season.

A 2-0 win at QPR secured West Brom the 2008 Championship title. Did you think you'd ever see the day?

28 v Aston Villa 3-1

Att: 20,399

14 January 1984

Albion	Aston Villa	Referee
Barron	Spink	A.W. Ward (London)
Whitehead	Williams	
Cowdrill	Gibson	
Luke	Evans	
McNaught	Bremner	
Bennett	Mortimer	
Zondervan	Curbishley	
Thompson	Shaw	
Regis	Withe	
Owen	McMahon	
Morley	Rideout	
Sub: Perry		

NOT FOR the first time in our history, Aston Villa were being a right pain in the whatsit. On the opening day of the season, the Baggies had played particularly well at Villa Park and scored three times. But Villa scored four. Then in the League Cup in November, the Baggies had competed fiercely but lost 2-1, finishing with nine men after some shocking decisions by referee Clive Thomas.

By the time his former club visited the Hawthorns for the return League match, manager Ron Wylie was under pressure. After four straight defeats, Albion had managed a win and a draw from their previous two fixtures but the malaise was deeper than results. Wylie was an odd managerial selection, lacking charisma and regularly accused of defensive football.

These perceptions didn't help attendances. Neither did losing at home to joke side Wolverhampton – one of only six wins the Staffordshire club would manage in forty-two games. For the players his loyalty to his deeply unpopular assistant Mike Kelly was their major concern. Thus the Albion ship was not a happy one as the old enemy came a-visiting. Pleasingly, table-topping ambitions were over for Villa these days and they were strictly mid-table fodder.

Just over 20,000 were at the Hawthorns for what would become the third highest attendance of the season. The bitterly cold weather may have deterred others and an irritating crosswind would create difficulties for the players throughout the 90 minutes.

The wind, combined with a downright soggy pitch, made for a difficult first half. Albion were on top, with Villa's 4-3-3 formation leaving a lot of gaps in midfield. Gary Owen and Tony Morley revelled in the space. Three times Villa's child-nightmare-inducing goalkeeper Spink had to be alert. It was perhaps typical of their luck against the Brummies that Albion weren't ahead.

It was also typical that Villa should take the lead against the run of play. Shortly after the re-start, Paul Barron pushed out a header from Rideout only for GARY SHAW to net from the rebound from point blank range. There were groans around three shivering sides of the Hawthorns. More moaning became audible as the Aston mob had the confidence to take the game to Albion. Villa's McMahon and Curbishley were winning their midfield battles. It was Gary Owen who turned the tide with a long-range effort that Nigel Spink brilliantly turned aside.

Now it was Albion taking the initiative and they had Morley to give them the width that Villa's system lacked. Yet despite their midfield superiority, Albion's big striking pair of Thompson and Regis found space very difficult to find. A chance finally came when Thommo broke free of his marker only for his back headed effort to hit the crossbar. Typical! It seemed that once again Villa would win the day, as their gleeful hordes pointed out from the Smethwick End. A blizzard descended on the Hawthorns as if the Gods were also displeased with the score and a few faint-hearted souls made for the exits.

With six minutes remaining, Villa's Evans made a mistake, presenting possession to THOMPSON. But the big man was still 50 yards from goal. No matter, he charged towards goal like a rampaging bull, ignoring the slippery surface. He dummied to pass to Morley, which confused final defender Curbishley before lobbing the onrushing Spink. It was a quite splendid goal and a right poke in the eye for Thompson's Dad, a Villa supporter.

Justice at last! Three sides of the Hawthorns whooped and hollered in union. After all the travails throughout the match, a draw was more than deserved. "Albion, Albion, Albion!" we bellowed frantically.

We were still celebrating the equaliser when THOMMO scored the winner. As journalist Leon Hickman had it: '…an unforgettable header from Clive Whitehead's sweeping pass to the far post. Thompson leapt, arched his body like a high diver and stretched that extra inch beyond a defender to wrongfoot Spink on the line.' The roar of success was primeval. Snow…who cares about snow now? Just in case the claret and blue mob had forgotten the score, we gave them a reminder. And another…Yes, it's definitely two…Ron Wylie would later describe the goal as Tommy Lawtonesque though admitted his players didn't know who Tommy Lawton was.

Meanwhile, a shattered Villa team were vainly trying to rescue a match which they thought they'd already won, pushing everybody forward to pressure the Albion goal. With barely a minute left, defender Bremner gave away the ball in the centre circle and big CYRILLE REGIS pounded away unmarked towards Spink's goal. Somehow although he hadn't scored for two months, the fairytale script dictated he would find the net. Sure enough, with complete confidence he rolled the ball past Spink. Tony Morley and Noel Luke were the first Albion men to pounce on him, followed by the rest. It was a glorious moment. Five minutes earlier Albion were a goal behind, but now victory was confirmed. A victory downright rubbed in.

If Albion supporters had a complaint, it was that they didn't have enough time to let the score sink in properly, let alone give full vent to a classic victory against the old foe. The Villa mob had gone – sliding out of the slippery exits as fast as possible. To the victors: a snow covered, bitterly cold victory scene and the urgent need to take in so much that had happened so quickly. Villa's manager Frank Barton was fuming: "There's no excuse for it. If players cannot roll their sleeves up after 84 minutes to keep what we have, you have to look at them."

The victory was roundly toasted in pubs all across the Black Country that night. The occasion needed commemorating as a quarter of a century later we still await another victory over Villa quite so decisive; or almost any victory at all. Let's hope Ron Wylie enjoyed his evening too because three weeks later he was out of a job.

v Rotherham United 2-0

Att: 8,059

1 May 1993

Albion	Rotherham United	Referee
Lange	Mercer	Paul Danson
McNally	Pickering	
Lilwall	Wilder	
Bradley	Banks	
Raven	Law	
Burgess	Richardson	
Hunt*	Hazel	
Hamilton	Varadi	
Taylor	Cunningham*	
Mellon**	Page	
Donovan.	Barrick	
Subs: Heggs*	Sub: Goater*	
Reid**		

WITH AN historic Black Country social institution taking on the genre of a Mad Hatters Tea Party in the late 1980s and early 1990s, the fury and indignation of its core asset – the supporters – hit spectacular heights. The five-times FA Cup Winners were beaten by non-League opposition for the first time for 80 years. WBA sunk to the English League's third tier for the first time and even worse, Gould was in command. The infamous coffin at Gay Meadow became an iconic symbol of decline during what ultimately became a day of protest. Eventually, even a bankrupt shed owner could take no more and the Albion revival started at last under Ardiles and Burkinshaw.

Heritage Albion was welcomed back with a delightful emphasis on attacking football. 17 home League matches were won with opponents often beaten before they took the field. The formula wasn't as successful away which is why the Baggies couldn't quite aspire to a top two finish. By the time the last regular away League match was upon us, WBA were in fourth place and regardless of the last two results, they would finish in that position. So Millmoor was a calm little harbour, a respite from the tense nervous seas all round. Or the Baggies' day off.

The end of season beachwear party was at its best during this era, when the need to introduce more fun and entertainment was paramount. We quickly sold our allocation of 4,500 tickets but the not so Merry Millers refused to increase the number even though much of their ground would remain empty. Their apparent attitude of resentment against WBA pointlessly persisted throughout the day.

It's hard to look menacing in flipflops and shorts yet all the pubs bar one were closed around the football ground. Thus many hundreds of beachwear-clad Baggies clutching inflatables assembled around the solitary open pub. The warm sunshine added to the mood of good humour and tolerance despite the rugby scrum at the bar. One enterprising supporter drove to a nearby off licence and filled his boot with cans which he re-sold in the car park. A collective game of 'spot the Rotherham fan' came to a ragged halt after the realisation dawned that there were none to spot.

Even outside Millmoor there were but a handful of home fans and even they were outnumbered by the ranks of unnecessary Police with dogs. Constabulary and grim industrial surroundings apart, one could appreciate Craig Shakespeare's observation that "it was more like Blackpool than Rotherham with all those white legs on display." The *Grorty Dick* sellers tried manfully to flog their wares but were constantly undermined by giggles at the mournful cries from the solitary vendor of 'Mi Whippet's Dead', the Rotherham offering. It was just that sort of day.

Inside Millmoor, the end terrace was jammed. So too the uncovered seats to the right – full of bright colours, lurid green alligators, inflatable women and jolly ditties such as "Where's the Beach?" Even the players look astonished. "It was amazing to watch from the pitch," admitted Darren Bradley. The rest of the ground was sparsely populated by 3,500 locals.

Rotherham United were safely in mid-table but felt the need to make an impression – mainly on Bob Taylor's legs. Page set the trend – booked for a heavy whack on Albion's top scorer within a minute. Richardson and Law also followed suit in the opening 45 minutes. There wasn't a lot of football being played; both sides created and missed one opening each. In the away end, collectively we weren't hugely bothered other than maintaining our proud record of not losing a theme match and that Bob ought to score. With 36 to his name he had a chance of beating the club record of 40 set by W.G. Richardson in 1936, albeit in far fewer matches. From his solitary opportunity in the second half, he put the ball wide of the post. Bob Taylor didn't need a bridge that season so his miss produced only loud choruses of his name: "Super, Super Bob…"

In the 63rd minute, Rotherham scored. Or rather they thought they had. Pickering squared for Varadi to beat Lange, but the linesman waved for offside. The ex-Albion man was furious and argued bitterly with referee Gunn.

Ardiles immediately used both his substitutes, asserting: "We had to make a change because we were struggling in defence." But weren't we always? As the new men entered the field of play, Varadi continued to argue and the referee, wearying of his moaning, sent him off. As the multi-hued contingent politely waved goodbye, two Rotherham fans ran onto the pitch while others fought between themselves at the home end.

Still, the changes (and the dismissal) gave Albion more impetus against frustrated and confused opposition. The eccentric Heggs was a mystery to his team-mates so the opposition had no hope of marking him. Ossie's men were prising open the door to goal at last. McNally spotted a gap and set up Super Bob but his shot was weak.

Albion forced a corner with two minutes remaining. Ian Hamilton's kick bounced crazily off a defender's head then deflected table-tennis-like off a second defender kindly to the feet of PAUL RAVEN, Albion's token defender. Raves didn't hesitate with a decisive volley that was in the net before the keeper could move. Within seconds, most of our team were on the fence celebrating with supporters. It meant nothing and yet so much at the same time.

The Police lined up a row of officers and dogs across our seated supporters. This forced them to stand and created unnecessary tension. So it was that their view was restricted when SUPER BOB finally got his goal in injury time, neatly set up by Heggs. Naturally the pair celebrated with their unique goal celebration. Mission accomplished!

The victory felt so special to both team and followers as they exchanged genuine mutual appreciation. The diversion was a blessed relief – now for the play-offs.

v Swansea City 2-0
Play-Off Semi-Final, Second Leg.
Att: 26,025. 19 May 1993

Albion	Swansea City	Referee
Lange	Freestone	Allan Gunn (Sussex)
McNally	Lyttle	
Lilwall	Jenkins	
Bradley	Walker	
Raven	Harris	
Strodder	Hayes*	
Hunt	Cullen	
Hamilton	Coughlin	
Taylor	McFarlane	
Mellon	Cornforth**	
Donovan	Legg	
Subs: Garner	Subs: West*	
Reid	Ford**	

"**W**EMBERLEE, WEMBERLEE, it's a place in London that we never get to see ..."

Albion finished the 1992/93 Division Two season with 85 points from 46 games, sometimes sufficient to land Championships, but not this one. The Stoke meat grinders won the title with 93 points with Bolton taking the other automatic spot. Albion had to compete in the play-offs for the first time. The prize of 'back door promotion' as it was unkindly called was almost eclipsed by the overwhelming potential of reaching Wembley. It had acquired near-mythical status for the frustrated Hawthorns regulars. Seemingly everyone else had visited the Twin Towers more recently than WBA. 1970 seemed a horribly long time ago. But there was one last barrier to overcome. As Ossie said with masterful understatement: "There is a little problem called Swansea." The scale of the problem was best gauged in the first leg where Albion never got to grips with the weather conditions, nerves or the flat-out Welsh. With the Baggies 2-0 down, hope came in the form of Burgess's selfless dive in for a 50/50 challenge in the Swansea goalmouth. His intervention gave Albion a desperately needed goal but he took such a whack he was sidelinded for the season.

One goal behind was not ideal but the situation could have been far worse. "The way the team is set up, we're always likely to score," declared Keith Burkinshaw. Coming from the man tasked with putting the brakes on Ossie, it sounded almost like a moan. West Bromwich could boast 19 different scorers to date, of which 4 were to finish in double figures. Apart from Super Bob's phenomenal scoring, Andy Hunt was averaging a goal a game. Were we not so savagely bitten by nerves, logic suggested Swansea ought to worry about playing the Baggies, not the other way round.

The visiting supporters were housed in the now unroofed Smethwick End, the first step of Trevor Summers's master plan to convert the ground into an all-seater. With remarkable prescience, Fred the Shed opted for a modest capacity, declaring: "Our maximum average gate will be between 22,000 and 25,000, even in the Premier League." He was universally ridiculed.

Phil Spector would have goggled at the Albion Wall of Sound, a raw throat-damaging cry of hope and fear which began before kick-off. Craig Shakespeare describes the atmosphere: "I have never heard noise like that at any football ground, let alone the Hawthorns. It is impossible to shut out that much noise and it served to fuel the players' passion." With that giant hand pushing at their back, Albion set about demolishing Swansea. The Swans' lead lasted only seven minutes. Bob Taylor made space down the left and set up ANDY HUNT to maintain his goal a game average. The roar…the celebration…it was beyond easy description though resembled a leaping, hugging, screaming mass of humanity.

There was better to follow. On 18 minutes, the Baggies cruised into the lead. Donovan's short corner, a trick from HAMILTON and the ball was in the net from an impossible angle. "I hit it without thinking about it. That's always best for me," the midfielder admitted later. More shrieking and near demonic celebrations followed which included the best ever BOING in the Brummie Road. The whole stand moved up and down 3 inches under the strain of 5,000 bouncing Baggies, necessitating WBA to call in safety experts the next day. *Dancing with tears in my eyes…*

Although Albion continued to dominate the Welsh club, a third goal eluded them. Time and time again, chances were created and wasted. But no-one was complaining at half-time except about the cramp brought about by keeping everything crossed.

Calamity struck early in the second half. Mickey Mellon lunged wildly at Coughlin and, having already been booked earlier, had to walk. Nervous tension turned into panic as Swansea streamed forward, seeking to take full advantage of the extra man. The situation became even worse when Raven was ordered to leave the field for attention to a head wound. Never has a trainer had so many people screaming at him at one time. With the Baggies down to nine, they could do no more than hang on desperately. Big striker McFarlane missed one chance then another as Raven's patching-up continued amid further screams of abuse. Our grip on Wembley was looking shaky; the six-minute absence of the central defender felt like sixty. Kevin Donovan: "When we were down to nine men, we were on the ropes but the sheer intensity of the crowd kept us going. There was no way we could lose for the fans' sake."

Even when the defender rejoined the fray, the game pattern had changed. The visitors were on top and for the first time we realised they had supporters too. Swansea brought on an extra striker in Colin West to make life more difficult, yet it was the ex-Albion man who was to inspire the Baggies. West foolishly retaliated to an Ian Hamilton tackle and was sent off. Oh the relief! We didn't know whether to jeer or cheer him so did both. Now we knew we could win and turned up the wick accordingly. Ian Hamilton remembers: "In the last 20 minutes, I could feel the tingle on my spine. I just knew we were going to win it then."

Arms around strangers, bellowing like your very life depended on it: "WEMBLEY, WEMBLEY…WE'RE THE FAMOUS WEST BROM-WICH ALBION AND WE'RE GOING TO WEMBLEY!" Kevin Donovan recalls the players' reaction: "We couldn't speak to each other on the pitch because you couldn't hear anything except the supporters. I will never play in another game like it."

Those minutes crawled by even as Albion were creating absurdly easy chances and still missing them. Howling at the referee, checking watches, howling again and then oh joy! – at last it was over and Albion were really, actually, truly going to Wembley. Tears were shed. Pitch invaded. Turf kissed. Players hugged. West Bromwich Albion were famous again.

v Port Vale 3-0

Play-off Final. Att: 53,471
30 May 1993

Albion	Port Vale	Referee
Lange	Musselwhite	Roger Milford (Bristol)
Reid	Aspin	
Lilwall	Kent*	
Bradley	Porter	
Raven	Swann	
Strodder	Glover	
Hunt*	Slaven	
Hamilton	Van der Laan**	
Taylor	Foyle	
McNally	Kerr	
Donovan	Taylor	
Sub: Garner*	Subs: Billing*	
	Cross**	

THE OLD axiom about enjoying the moment has rarely been more true. Even as he prepared his team for the big day, contract-less Ardiles had been discreetly tapped up by Tottenham and knew he would go. He kept the information to himself. Anyway, supporters' attention was focused on getting their hands on small but perfectly formed pieces of paper.

Port Vale's childish attitude to selling play-off final tickets did their credibility no favours. Unable to sell three quarters of their allocation, nevertheless they refused to hand any over to the Baggies. Some small scale trading was arranged via Potteries-based Albionites but there was a limit to how many times they could visit without detection. Vale supporters who could be bothered had an easy time buying tickets. At the Hawthorns, literally a mile-long queue formed as the group at the front knew exactly where they wanted to sit and weren't prepared to compromise. Meanwhile the rest of the 6,000-strong queue waited impatiently for a minimum of four hours.

What is it about Wembley that dictates a lemming-like urge to arrive early in such a depressing and unwelcoming area? Perhaps after 23 years, such haste can be forgiven as the Albion army took over Wembley Way and every local pub from early morning. *Are we really here? At Wembley? Albion?*

The difference in the support was striking at the old stadium for the TV audience. Over 42,000 completely filled one half while at the other, Vale's pathetic number sat leper-like in splendid isolation. Albion midfielder Bernie McNally describes the scene: "All you could see was blue and white and yellow and green. It was absolutely fantastic and you just kind of knew this is our day today." The Albion coach carefully nosed through an endless sea of well wishing, applauding supporters while their Vale counterparts were welcomed by exactly two supporters plus a Division of the Black Country army hollering "Who are yer?"

Collective tension gripped tensely and refused to let go. After all, Vale could play a bit and had already beaten WBA twice in the League. Who could say how damaging failure would be? (It would be 15 years before Swansea were to recover from their play-off exit.) Supporters tried to ease their nerves through vocal support. Although impressive, the noise levels rarely matched those of the Swansea match – too big a ground and too many part-timers among the regulars.

Not surprisingly, the early action was tentative and nervous. Both of the best chances fell to Kevin Donovan but the midfielder, although in double figures for the season, missed them both. Rational behaviour had long gone out of the window so he was on the receiving end of some very pointed stick. Even the most cynical could see that the Baggies were dominant yet we had no proof of this on the scoreboard. The old wounds of semi-final defeats in '78 and '82 itched. When Donovan missed a third opportunity, the terrace language became ripe.

To this day, both Vale supporters maintain the sending off of Swan in the 59th minute turned the game. In truth, the tide was already against them. The player simply had to walk as without his crude intervention, Bob Taylor would have been clear on goal. Swan's hasty departure from the pitch, aided by voluminous choruses of "Cheerio", felt mightily significant. The best passing team in the Division now had more space and the pressure was on Vale. They had survived for only ten minutes when Strodder hit the post from a corner. Although Musselwhite fisted the ball clear, Nicky Reid chipped it back in and ANDY HUNT so beautifully found the top corner with his head. It was simply one of the best ever moments to be a Baggie. We screamed. We shouted. We hugged. We cried. This was our time.

Neutrals probably believed promotion was decided by that single goal. Albion supporters knew our defence better than that. We needed more. Thus our joy was unbounded seven minutes from time when Donovan set up NICKY REID who blasted his effort past the Vale keeper for his one and only Albion goal. Then we knew and so did the whole world: "We are Going Up…" There was healing balm in those words…Woking, Bath, Gould…those old wounds being massaged. Oh and relief too by the shovel load.

We didn't need a third goal but DONOVAN certainly did. Close to full-time, he finished off a loose ball in the penalty box and then offered a goalscorer's slide of delight in front of the photographers. Promotion here we come. There was time to bring on Simon Garner for a couple of minutes as a nod towards his contribution over the season but sadly no swansong minutes for Gary Robson despite his 12 years of service.

To this day, Darren Bradley remains the only Albion first-team captain to lift a trophy at Wembley in the last four decades. The post-match scenes were everything Albion supporters had ever dreamed about. Bernie McNally describes the celebrations: "I remember at the final whistle and we were all celebrating, I felt a bit like Nobby Stiles. I actually said to the lads, 'Shall we go round again?' and most of them said, 'Oh no, that would be a bit much'. When you get to 32 years of age you realise you might not be there again." Keith Burkinshaw apparently never had any doubts: "I always knew we would beat Vale because we had better players."

After endless joyful volleys of "We are Going Up", there was a change of direction for a little guy from South America standing behind the goal. "Ossie's Barmy Army…" The same words over and over again, a wall of noise. The emphasis on the first word was slightly different and slightly louder each time. "*Ossie's* Barmy Army…" At that moment, his popularity knew no bounds. But there was an embarrassment about Ossie's smile. He knew…

v Wolves 3-2

Att: 25,615

5 September 1993

Albion	Wolves	Referee
Lange	Stowell	P.L. Foakes (Clacton)
Fereday*	Rankine	
Lilwall	Thompson	
Bradley	Cook	
Raven	Blades	
Burgess	Venus	
Hunt	Birch	
Hamilton	Thomas	
Garner**	Bull*	
O'Regan	Kelly	
Donovan.	Keen.	
Subs: Strodder*	Sub: Regis*	
Ampadu**		

THE POST-Wembley season felt like an exciting new beginning, even though we'd only been absent from the country's second tier for only two seasons. Ardiles had sadly departed but the euphoria of promotion carried us through the first few fixtures. Form was reasonable with five points picked up in four games. Had not bloody Stoke been among the four opponents, the points tally would have been even higher. Game five was widely perceived to be one of the best parts of promotion, the chance to renew hostilities with the local rag and bone men – the Tatters of Wolverhampton. Quite what the rush was to take on a side that we'd been unable to beat for 11 years wasn't made clear... or maybe that was the rush.

To achieve this feat would surely require input from our main man Bob Taylor. But including the tail end of the previous season, seven games had passed without a Super Bob goal, his worst spell since joining WBA. "I'm more disappointed with myself than anything else," he explained. The King advised him: "Stop trying so hard where it matters." A couple of days later, Bob heeded the wise words and scored twice against Southend. This was a timely boost barely a week before the horse and cart hordes trotted along. In another positive sign Wolves manager Graham Turner, himself a veteran defender, lamented that his back four couldn't stop a pig in an entry, stating: "We desperately need to improve the defence." For a club backed by an open cheque book, this was comical indeed. Albion spent £250,000 on new players in the summer. The Haywood mob spent eight times that amount on just four men – Thomas, Keen, Birch and Cook.

The fixture was scheduled for a Sunday, then a novelty. Albion supporters dared to hope – with the potential of Donovan and Hunt prompting Bob Taylor. And then Bob caught the pox from his wife Lesley (of the chicken variety naturally). The man we most wanted at the Hawthorns was told to stay away. Rumours of a cameo appearance shaking hands in the away dressing room were sadly inaccurate.

Taylor's late cry off was the second setback for the Baggies. The West Midlands Police set the tone by objecting to an alcohol licence to serve post-match drinks in the executive boxes. The licence was refused on the grounds that it was not an important occasion. Hmmm ... Boldly unafraid of rioting by Chief Executives in suits, Albion offered a free post-match bar.

The bulk of the 25,000 crowd went without alcohol, other than a few who were either resourceful or desperate. Pity – Dutch courage is invaluable for such occasions. 12 minutes into the game, a stiff drink was urgently required as with horrible predictability, STEVE BULL connected perfectly with a Paul Birch centre. Albion followers were wretchedly familiar with this script.

The team was less familiar, with only Darren Bradley left from the last derby in April 1991. But within four minutes, they'd drawn level. In an extraordinary sight, one centre-half Daryl Burgess crossed from the right wing to his defensive partner PAUL RAVEN who headed home. Ardiles would have been proud of such all-out attack.

The moneybags visitors were forced onto the attack but found Albion's midfield, in which Kieran O'Regan snapped away furiously, to be particularly resilient. Bull only had one more chance which Lange bravely smothered. O'Regan had an opportunity of his own in the Wolves box but fatally hesitated. Naturally tempers became strained and the unstable Paul Cook was lucky to stay on the pitch after kicking Kevin Donovan. This being a derby, Donovan kicked him back.

There was no doubt that the Tatters were on top and Albion's position was becoming perilous. So DARREN BRADLEY did something about it. Playing an extravagant one-two he strode confidently into the opposition half and let fly from fully 30 yards. Stowell got nowhere near the ball. It was a goal to make supporters gape in wonderment first rather than cheer, though we did manage both. With typical understatement, his manager Keith Burkinshaw described the strike being "as good a goal as you'll ever get." To this day, Bradders's greatest moment is immortalised on YouTube.

The unopposed Goal of the Season deserved to be a winner. The Tatters decreed otherwise. They pierced Albion's back four with GEOFF THOMAS touching in a header from Venus. All square again and still 30 minutes to play.

Steve Bull sunk to the ground, an injury compelling his ultimate removal from the pitch. Following common practice at the time, Albion supporters cheered wildly as their tormentor was removed. There was another far more warm cheer for his replacement Cyrille Regis. His accolade remains a unique honour for anyone wearing a Wolves shirt. Fortunately he was not to try his hosts' hospitality by scoring.

The next and mercifully concluding goal came from the Baggies. Kwame Ampadu, on for the flagging Garner, made one of his rare significant contributions with an accurate centre which KEVIN DONOVAN delightfully headed past Stowell to rapturous acclaim. It was Donovan's fifth goal of the season and one of his best ever. His running had frequently troubled Turner's back division who had now conceded nine goals in three matches.

Albion were determined not to concede again and without Bull the visitors had no cutting edge. The final minutes were played out with the visiting support on the receiving end of 11 years of hurt. For all their much vaunted wealth, the Staffordshire mob were beaten by the Baggies and their frustration was written large across the entire Smethwick End. Journalist Leon Hickman wrote: 'Wolves are a cheque that has not been cashed.' Keith Burkinshaw preferred to talk of the "terrific self-belief" from his team, a description now shared with Albion supporters whose team was fifth in the table and without that old gold monkey on their backs. We dared to dream of better times over a pint or six that evening...

v Wolves 2-1

Att: 28,039

26 February 1994

Albion	Wolves	Referee
Naylor	Stowell	Robbie Hart (Darlington)
Burgess	Thompson	
Edwards	Venus	
Bradley	Masters	
Mardon	Blades	
Raven*	Shirtliff	
Hunt**	Dennison	
McNally	Ferguson	
Donovan	Regis*	
Smith	Kelly	
Taylor:	Keen.	
Subs: Parsley*	Sub: Mills*	
Fereday**		

R ARELY HAVE pre-match events so influenced the outcome of a match. Relations between the two clubs were at an all-time low, prompted by the two Club Chairmen displaying all the gravitas of drunken blokes in a pub. Haywood Junior declared that the Baggies would only receive 2,500 of the 27,000 tickets available. His justification that he could fill the ground with his own supporters completely missed the point. Wolves received double that number at the Hawthorns and had given a gentlemen's agreement to return the gesture. We should have realised that Wolves and gentlemen have very little in common. WBA compounded the grievance with shoddy ticket selling practices, for which they were notorious at the time. In addition, Chairman Summers was firing his usual Hyde Park Corner cringeworthy statements in all directions.

Albion under Keith Burkinshaw had struggled in the League and had only just won their first away match. To misquote a famous newsreader: 'We were as mad as hell and we weren't going to take it any more.' Having been messed around, wound up and abused, both team and supporters wanted this game so badly. The gallant 2,500 had a narrow sliver of the South Bank – with an even narrower divide from the frothing at the mouth

Wolves supporters. They were still hurting from losing 3-2 at the Hawthorns back in September despite their bankrolled status. They were the club with the money and they expected hard-up Albion to curl up and die. After all, WBA hadn't won at Molineux since 1982. Meanwhile back at the Hawthorns, 6,800 supporters prepared for an afternoon screaming at a very large television screen.

Wolves began menacingly, particularly through the elusive Dennison on the wing. In the away end, we feared the worst. After 19 minutes Wolves were ahead, KEEN drilling home low to Naylor's left from 15 yards following a kerfuffle at a long throw from the right. It hurt and as the uncouth hordes bellowed belligerently in triumph, the situation looked ominous.

Without the sidelined Bull (oh joy!), Graham Turner's side weren't that much of a threat. Indeed, their front men David Kelly and big Cyrille both had reason to be favourably inclined towards the Baggies. For all Wanderers' muscle and workrate, Albion's back line had too much pace and class for them. Paul Mardon was at his imperious best, arguably his finest ever game in an Albion shirt. He was strong in the air and immaculate with his distribution.

The highly welcome Albion equaliser owed much to Bernie McNally's determination (the Irishman was not exactly famed for aggressive tackling) as he tore into Keen. The ball squirted free from his shuddering challenge, handily to the feet of SUPER BOB who was lurking on the edge of the box. It was duly despatched clinically into the net. We love that man. All afternoon we'd felt as if we were taking on the whole world and had lustily backed the side. Now there was something to celebrate, vocal efforts were racked up to throat damaging levels. Meanwhile the surrounding home mob smouldered with fury. We gallant few had a football club to represent. Oh for a decibel reader in the away section. This was personal.

If the 25,000 home followers thought an equaliser was painful, there was worse to come. Three minutes later, Bradley delivered a gorgeous cross from a free kick wide on the right and MARDON underlined his international status by thundering home the Baggies' second with his head. Joy unconfined. 'Mards' disappeared under a heap of celebrating players. There just aren't sufficient words to describe the impact of two goals against the Tatters in under 200 seconds.

Predictably, the maddened old gold stormed at their guests in the second half. The Stars in Stripes stood tall and worked their socks off to retain their shape and composure. The team were at one with the supporters, fuelled by the sense of injustice. The gallant few bellowed their defiance and their opinions on all matters Wolverhampton. All around us, the hordes were getting angrier and angrier.

For the last 20 minutes, full back Parsley had to stand in for the injured Raven as a makeshift central defender. Sensing redemption, the home side reverted to their 1950s roots, hoisting long balls and attempting to batter their way through. Trying to protect their lead, the Albion men were defending deeper and deeper. The last ten minutes seemed endless with Wolves forcing corner after corner. Somehow, the patched up West Bromwich side hung in there.

It was a gutsy Albion showing with outstanding teamwork and the utmost calm under pressure. Bruiser Naylor pulled out one marvellous, clinging save at full stretch. This was an awkward bobbling shot by Albion shareholder Kelly from the edge of the box. At the final whistle Albion had ridden out the storm (albeit a generally toothless one) to secure a rapturous triumph.

The entire team capered and hugged each other in front of the screaming, bellowing Albion support. There's nothing to match the excitement of an unexpected away win against the odds – particularly in a derby. Not only were the three points invaluable to us, that win denied to the Dingles ultimately meant they missed out on the play-offs.

Dreadful scenes followed when the jubilant away support attempted to leave the stadium. Volleys of stones and lumps of concrete were hurled by hooligans allowed to get within chucking distance of the away exit. After much confusion, the police ushered the away following back into the ground for a 45-minute siege while they dealt with the hooligan element.

Thankfully, scenes on that scale have never been repeated but there was a long term price to pay. Albion supporters of a nervous disposition have not returned to Molineux while the subsequent mass-policing since regularly causes inconvenience all round.

v Portsmouth 1-0
Att:17,629
8 May 1994

Albion	Portsmouth	Referee
Lange	Knight	David Elleray (Harrow)
Strodder	Dobson	
Darton	Powell	
Ashcroft*	Gittens	
Parsley	Pethick	
Raven	Stimson	
Hunt	Chamberlain	
Hamilton	Hall	
Taylor	Doling*	
Donovan	Wood	
McNally.	Kristensen	
Subs: Mellon*	Sub: Burton*	

S EASON 93/94 became a frustrating campaign for promoted Albion. A reasonable start was followed by indifferent form. Only two points from the fifteen available in April meant the Stars in Stripes had to win two out of the last three matches to retain their status. Grimsby were pipped 1-0 but the second match was lost 3-2 at Luton on a quagmire of a pitch. This was a bruising encounter and cost us not just points but players too. For the now genuinely must-win fixture at Fratton Park, WBA were without five regulars – Burgess, Mardon, Edwards, Bradley plus first choice keeper Stuart 'Bruiser' Naylor. This was a simple three-way fight between Albion, Blues and Oxford. As Sir Alan Sugar didn't say: 'Two of you will be fired.' The scenario was complicated but to be sure of retaining their status the Baggies had to win.

Fortunately Portsmouth were also missing half a dozen regulars. Pompey had nothing to play for yet they were at home with all the pressures that entailed, and with only two away wins, the Albion team didn't travel well. But the supporters did! Fratton Park was then primarily terraced and Pompey saw no need to impose an all-ticket restriction. Thus thousands of the Albion army were on the move south. The motorway service station where the A34 meets the M4 was swamped with Black

Country people in beachwear. So much so that other supporters imme-diately cancelled their pit stop and kept going. Just how would all these people get in?

On arrival, only fans with seat tickets felt able to sup a soothing pre-match pint. Everyone else joined a snaking queue which stretched around several street corners. Forward momentum was so ponderous that the editors of *Grorty Dick* fanzine easily sold out. They then walked the queue once more selling Portsmouth fanzines on behalf of their nervous editor and sold out again. One nice touch was the injured Daryl Burgess wandering among nerve-wracked queuing Baggie people, chatting merrily to the faithful. A bit like a commander reviewing his troops.

As kick-off time approached, the full size of the Albion support was evident. The entire away end was a heaving, boinging mass of beachwear. Earlier in a fit of pre-relegation schadenfreude they donated beach balls of various sizes and descriptions to the players in response to despairing Pompey pleas for the return of their practice balls. 'You got us into this mess, you play with THEM' seemed to be the message. The away end was inadequate. In desperation, officials opened up a poorly-segregated section adjacent to the home support to cram in more visitors – a mistake as shortly before 3pm, trouble flared and kick-off was delayed by four minutes as Police waded in. Portsmouth fans resented being outnum-bered on their own ground by travelling support estimated at 10,000.

The smell of fear was overwhelming. Already weakened by absentees, Albion had the jitters and made error after error. Word that the Bluenoses were already ahead added to the anxiety. A new song was coined, one which is still heard today. A Black Country version of *Go West – Go West Bromwich Albion*.

Shortly before the interval came the joyful breakthrough. Taylor found Hamilton on the left wing. Hammy takes up the story: "I managed to get a cross in on my left foot and LEE ASHCROFT, who was the shortest player on the pitch managed to head it in." Lee had never previously scored with his head. The irritated home fans invaded the pitch and the situation became tense. Once order was re-established, referee Elleray blew for half-time, five minutes early.

The second half was about lead retention, especially with Blues and Oxford winning. Portsmouth seemed more irritated than concerned (they had four bookings to their name) but Albion were just one mistake or one effort on goal from oblivion – thankfully it wasn't the 53rd minute effort from Smethwick-born Hall which required a brilliant save from Lange, not to mention two goal-line clearances by Strodder. Watches were checked and re-checked. Some of the travelling faithful turned their backs, unable to watch.

News of a Tranmere equaliser against Blues brought some relief. A point might now be enough. As if encouraged by this event, Albion pushed their opponents back and had chances to make the game safe … but just couldn't finish them.

The last few minutes were no place for the faint hearted. There were craven delaying tactics by Taylor, Hunt, Hamilton and others. Albion's defenders were so jittery. Blues were ahead once more so it was win or bust. *The Lord's My Shepherd* was sung, this time with a fervour that was awe-inspiring in its intensity. More checks of watches and finally … finally Elleray blew his whistle for the last time.

This prompted a pitch invasion of unparalleled proportions, with beachwear-clad Baggies and their inflatable toys pouring onto the pitch for their own version of a Sunday Service. Best of all was a heartfelt "We are Staying Up" bellowed to the skies. There was no room left on the pitch for the Albion team to make a return so the massed ranks managed perfectly well without them. Even better news was that Ashcroft's goal had relegated our City neighbours on goals scored. Not since Oldham had the end of a game felt so beautiful.

The Portsmouth police, concerned that an element of the home support had tried to get on the pitch, were keen to usher the Albion army out of Fratton Park and out of town. To reinforce the point, every turn-off and every service station was blocked for 60 miles north. It was a slightly sour ending to a Dunkirk season.

Meanwhile the Albion players were having their own celebrations in their double decker coach. The alcohol flowed freely and high jinks ensued. The toilet mysteriously had a lock on the outside and predictably manager Keith Burkinshaw was locked in. Having tried reason which failed dismally he resorted to kicking his way through the door. His tired and emotional players were distinctly unconcerned about his complaints.

v **Brescia** 1-0

Anglo-Italian Cup. Att: 18,000
13 December 1995

Albion	Brescia	Referee
Naylor	Cusin	C.Wilkes (Gloucester)
Burgess	Adani	
Smith	Bonometti	
Darby	Luzardi	
Edwards	Mezzanotti	
Raven	E.Filippini	
Donovan*	A.Filippini	
Gilbert	Volpi	
Taylor	Campolonghi*	
Rees**	Barollo**	
Hamilton.	Saurini.	
Subs: Hargreaves*	Subs: Lunini*	
Coldicott**	Neri**	

TRAVELLING ABROAD to follow your team is a unique refinement of football support – at no other time does camaraderie and mutual support reach such a peak. Everyone has a story to tell, an experience to share and a place to recommend. The Anglo-Italian Cup, which staggered along for a few seasons in the 1990s was generally ill-viewed but provided hugely enjoyable travelling experiences for Baggie people.

Albion's match against Serie B opposition was their final one in their group, and with a win, draw and defeat to their name, there was a slight chance of qualifying by finishing in the top four. This minor issue had an extra incentive – finishing that high would eliminate bloody Stoke from the competition. But the imperative was a short foreign break with good mates. Albion had lost the previous eight domestic games in a row so no-one was getting carried away.

Brescia themselves had little to offer so the away following plumped for fully savouring the delights of either Venice or Milan as the venue lay roughly between the two. The clans gathered at Brescia railway station during the day of the match before catching a number 4 bus to the stadium. Snow fell from midday and didn't stop; over an inch lay on the ground two hours before kick-off. Naturally, there were concerns about a postponement. "We ain't f*****g coming again!" was a common loud comment.

The away support was corralled together in the rear half of the main stand, the only covered section of the ground. Albion's 100+ strong following was splendid in the circumstances outnumbering the 80 home supporters. "You're supposed to be at home" followed by a rousing chorus of "Did you come in a taxi?" were predictable if a little lost in the translation. And still the snow fell. Four groundstaff with brooms busily swept the touchlines and vaguely cleared a token area of the penalty box. Referee Clive Wilkes, previously infamous for disallowing a hat-trick of Bob Taylor goals at Bristol Rovers in the League Cup, made the common-sense decision that as everybody has travelled, they would play. Not so 100 miles up the road where Reggiana v bloody Stoke was called off, 30 minutes before kick-off.

The whole spectacle was just so bizarre it was impossible not to smile despite the cold. Even the Albion team all managed impressive grins for the photographers (two supporters gleefully stepping in for the absent professionals). It was the strongest available side too, unlike the home club who fielded only five of the eleven from the previous League match.

It was naturally unfair, given the surface, to expect talent to flourish. The *Gazzetta dello Sport* spoke of *'sereta glaciale'*, *'impossibili condizioni'* and *'equilibro problematico'*. The overwhelming impression was of fragmented farce, 22 footballers doing their best to muster some semblance of football. The diminutive Dave Gilbert gave a perfect impression of striding down a white staircase whenever his little legs tried to move forward. Smudger Smith had problems of his own – a cynical elbow in the face. Meanwhile, from the sidelines, the irascible Alan Buckley irritably shouted: "This isn't a football match."

The Baggies support, determined to enjoy themselves, were in spectacular form. You had to be there to fully appreciate the inventive humour behind chants like "You only drink frothy coffee" and the off the wall nature of concerted cries about Mussolini's weight and parentage. The tiny home following remained silent. And then one of the London Baggies remembered a song he'd heard at the Milan v Napoli game the previous Sunday. Onemental tweak... and: "Brescia, Brescia, *vaffanculo!*" The Brescia tifosi resembled an ant's nest stirred with a stick. Clearly, the

English sense of humour and ribald rivalry was lost upon them. The more they raged the louder and longer the ditty was sung.

Meanwhile half-time came and went, which Baggie followers enlivened by pelting the Albion photographer with snowballs. The Albion substitutes were throwing frozen missiles at each other before picking on the ground staff instead. It's football Jim, but not as we know it.

And so the players battled on gamely despite the worsening conditions. 'Bruiser' Naylor made a couple of decent saves as the Italians pressed. Yet all the vocal support was for the visitors with a heartening extended version of "Blue and White Army". Just avoiding a defeat would suffice for most, numbed by both cold and successive League losses. The match was heading for stalemate (snowmate?) until three minutes from time when a long ball from Hamilton found Bob Taylor. SUPER BOB was clear through on keeper Cusini and his prod saw the ball roll tantalisingly slowly through the snow, over the line and come to rest in the net where yet more flakes settled on it. A celebratory "Boing… Boing… " was ragged but most heartfelt. In a few seconds, Albion had not just won a game, they'd reached the quarter-finals. Bloody Stoke were out.

When the referee blew for the last time, the players and the substitutes leaped in the air, hugging madly and all seemed genuinely pleased to win. Encouraged by management, the whole team came over to the away end, snowballs in hand. For several minutes, snow flew madly before the outnumbered stars in stripes retreated to the dressing room.

A memorable evening and there was more to follow. 40 Albion supporters were crammed onto an already nearly full last bus on the insistence of the Police and escorted into town. The passengers looked terrified despite our fumbling efforts to reassure them. The same force later made a through train stop to get a group of Milan-bound Black Country folk out of town. For the rest, a kindly bar owner provided classic free Italian food as we drank his bar dry.

In the wider context, the Ango-Italian Cup was a tinpot competition or as Darren Bradley put it, "a complete waste of time." But it was also a unique shared experience where supporters and players worked as one to overcome the odds.

v Leicester City 2-1

Att: 17,888

9 April 1996

Albion	Leicester City	Referee
Spink	Poole	J. Cruikshank
Burgess	Grayson	(Hartlepool)
Mardon	Whitlow	
Raven	Watts	
Coldicott*	Walsh	
Sneekes	Izzet	
Hamilton	Lennon	
Butler	Taylor	
Nicholson	Claridge	
Taylor	Roberts*	
Hunt	Heskey	
Sub: Gilbert*	Sub: Robins*	

ALBION HAD three seasons in one during the nine months of the 1995/96 season. Initially, the side maintained the momentum given to them by a successful finish from 1994/95 when Buckley's disciplined team moved well clear of relegation danger. By mid-October, Albion were in the highly unlikely position of being second in the League. The side were clearly overachieving but what fans didn't anticipate was a wretched run of one point from fourteen matches. The Baggies slid miserably from second top to second bottom. A team bonding session around Tony Brien's stag night finally inspired Albion to their first win in months. But the pressure was now on to stay in the Division. Through grit and disciplined performances, Buckley's Albion ground out a series of positive results to help their relegation fight.

The arrival of one Richard Sneekes gave the side much needed flair and a link between midfield and attack. The new midfielder scored six times in his first seven matches yet still the threat of relegation lingered and only six games remained. The next opponents were Leicester City. City, only relegated from the Premier League the previous season had promotion ambitions but had just lost their manager Brian Little. City had brought in a young Martin O'Neill to replace him in the hot seat. Early results had not been totally positive and the Filbert Street regulars were becoming restless.

On paper City's array of strikers – Steve Claridge, Emile Heskey, Iwan Roberts and Mark Robins – was formidable. Albion's 3-5-2 formation normally made them defensively sound but not against this illustrious bunch of workers and bashers. Still, the evening fixture was only 50 miles away and the presence of Sneekes made Buckley's side exciting to watch so the travelling numbers in the infamous bus shelter stand were very impressive. After all, didn't Buckley say: "We're not going to Leicester looking for a draw if that's what people think."? The stadium bookies were offering an extraordinarily generous 9/1 on Richard Sneekes to score the first goal. Word spread quickly and the queue was both long and patient.

The tail end of the bookies queue undoubtedly missed kick-off. The referee blew his whistle and then 11 seconds later blew it again as Roberts went down with an injury and it quickly became apparent that the toothless one would take no further part. On came Mark Robins so City's loss didn't seem so great. Heskey was already bullying his marker, Coldicott. Our 'Stace' was a workaholic and a decent marker but being on the short side, struggled against an opponent that big. Albion supporters quickly feared the worst but then were up and hollering as astonishingly the visitors took the lead. RICHARD SNEEKES shot spectacularly from 30 yards and memorably the ball lodged in the stanchion. City's Poole pulled the ball out, looking quite disgusted. Once our arms went down, up went the betting slips waving in the air. "That's my gas bill paid!" yelled one pragmatic supporter happily, in between the chant of "Sneekes, Sneekes!" The player himself admitted: "I would have been just as happy with a tap-in."

The 17th minute goal gave the visitors something to hang on to and this was their clear intention despite the manager's words. City quickly pressed and Albion's 3-5-2 became an unashamed 5-3-2. Leicester fortunately became their own worst enemy, too aware of their less than supportive supporters. Alan Buckley could see the danger signs: "Sneekes scored a fabulous goal but then we stopped passing the ball and keeping it, for an hour we were disappointing." Quite true. Consequently in the 57th minute, City at last made their pressure tell with MARK ROBINS notching the equaliser. Now it was all hands to the pumps. Claridge missed. Then Robins missed.

Buckley was forced into team changes. On came Dave Gilbert, off went Stacy Coldicott. Albion went 4-4-2 while the eminently more suited Daryl Burgess took over marking Heskey. West Bromwich were transformed. Ball artist Gilbert demanded the ball and kept it. His presence lifted the whole side just at the time when Leicester, with their big spearhead now tightly marked, became shackled and frustrated. The home fans were even more irritated, thus increasing the pressure on their favourites. A hard-won point seemed ours for the taking. The remaining time slowly eased away as Albion probed tentatively at their hosts, nibbling at their defence while keen to retain possession. The Filbert mob continued to moan.

The 90 minutes expired, only the referee knew how much more play there would be. Albion continued to attack cautiously and with 93 minutes gone, won a corner at the far end of the ground from the away support. Surely this was another chance to waste more time? No. Albion went for it with the central defenders pushed into the box. Richard Sneekes took the corner and found PAUL RAVEN who calmly headed in his sixth goal of the season! "The Raven Swoops!" screamed the *Radio WM* commentator. He wasn't the only screamer. To pinch a last minute winner at a promotion chasing side was quite marvellous and the Boinging bellowing celebrations were long and loud. The goalscorer confessed later: "I think a few of us would have settled for a point so to get all three is tremendous."

The bonus win gave Albion 51 points and effective safety from relegation. Leicester City were marooned in eighth place and their supporters furious. They took it in turns to vent their spleen on the local radio phone-in, each call being a variant of a theme that Martin O'Neill wasn't up to the job and should go. Seven weeks later, as O'Neill accepted rapturous accolades from supporters after his City side had just won the play-offs, he replied with: "I've got a tape of the supporters' phone-in after the Albion game. Would you like to hear it?" Meanwhile, buoyed by their win at Filbert Street, Albion remained unbeaten for the rest of the season, finishing in a highly respectable 11th place.

v Charlton Athletic 2-0
Att: 22,101
7 May 2000

Albion	Charlton Athletic	Referee
Jensen	Kiely	D. Pugh
Lyttle	Barness	
Butler	Konchesky	
Carbon	Parker	
Clement	Rufus	
Flynn	Tiler	
Sneekes	Newton*	
Santos*	Kinsella	
van Blerk	Hunt	
Taylor	Svensson**	
Quinn**	Robinson.	
Subs: Oliver*	Subs: Stuart*	
Evans**	Salako**	

WHEN GARY Megson gleefully accepted the Albion hot seat in March 2000, it really was a big job. A deadly combination of the clueless Brian Little, equally lackadaisical players, a shortage of time and low confidence created by only one win in sixteen matches made up a wildly careering juggernaut. Making quick, tough decisions, Megson weeded out underperforming players and brought in five hard-working professionals on deadline day: Des Lyttle, Neil Clement, Georges Santos, Tony Butler and a return for Super Bob Taylor. Some progress was made in a series of scrappy matches, but an embarrassing Easter Saturday 2-1 defeat to Walsall felt like the final straw. Defeat to Walsall is always embarrassing but particularly when they're your relegation rivals. Still Albion recovered to ground out a 2-1 victory over Grimsby and grimly defended a 0-0 draw at QPR to go into the last home game with their fate just about in their own hands. The scenario was stark. With the two clubs locked on 46 points, Albion had to at least equal Walsall's result to retain their League status. The Saddlers were away to play-off hopefuls Ipswich while the Baggies had the equally difficult-looking task of playing against the Champions Charlton Athletic at home.

Before kick-off, there was much speculation as to how bothered Charlton would be. Would the Londoners fight or not? Aggressive midfielder Sean Flynn advised his team-mates to "kick 'em, punch 'em, do anything to 'em." Typical diplomatic Flynn. But there was only room for one uber-aggressive person in the dressing room and that's the manager, as James Quinn noted: "He [Megson] would rip your head off if he was allowed to." Megson's approach was warmly welcomed by supporters. This was no time for niceties.

The first half was tense. Horribly tense. Charlton had decided not to be nice, with three of their men booked, two of them for clobbering Albion's powerful midfielder Santos. Amid the tension, nervous Albion carved out two decent opportunities. Des Lyttle cleverly slid the ball through to Sneekes who was making one of his classic runs from deep. The Dutchman did everything right before rolling the ball two feet wide of the post as the onrushing Dean Kiely narrowed the angle. Cue gnashing of teeth at the Birmingham Road End.

Five minutes later, Matt Carbon hit the base of the post from a set piece. That's as in hitting the post with the ball, a distinction not always clear to the eccentric defender. Although there was no goal to celebrate, Walsall hadn't scored either so the Baggies were just about holding their own above the drop line. More positively, perhaps fearful of the fulminating Megson, the Albion back four were rock solid. But this wasn't an end in itself; the defence was just a starting platform. As local journalist Phil Gordos put it: 'Albion were transformed into a team full of passion, bright ideas and flair.'

Albion's top goalscorer Lee Hughes was injured. Kevin Kilbane, the second top goalscorer was sold in December to keep the bank happy. Laughably (if the situation wasn't so serious) the highest scorer on the pitch was Sean Flynn with five to his name. The big question on everyone's lips was who was going to find the net? With only a few minutes of the second half gone, Albion enjoyed a huge breakthrough. But not in the Black Country. Ipswich had obligingly scored, so with Walsall losing the Baggies now had some insurance. The news whipped hurricane-like around the seats and quickly a roar of raw encouragement mounted around the Hawthorns. Curiously, it was the Londoners who responded. ANDY HUNT found himself with the ball at his feet with only Brian Jensen to beat. Dashing hopes that he'd do his old playing mates a favour, the Beast only just got one big hand to the former Albion man's shot. Cheers Andy.

Megson brought on an additional central striker to bolster our attack. Mickey Evans had only scored three League goals but the desperation was showing. WBA badly needed relief.

In the 65th minute, they got it. A badly directed Albion free kick didn't find a man in stripes but the ball kindly dropped to SNEEKES standing just feet inside the penalty box. "Shoot!" was the cry. But to cries of anguish who recalled his miss in the first half, the midfielder held possession. Very calmly, he dribbled across the goalmouth ignoring the howls of frustration. Deliberately, he beat Kiely low on his left hand side and turned for a Sneekes glory run. From plonker to hero in just ten seconds! "What the bloody hell are you … YESSSS!" The relief was simply overwhelming. With the hypocrisy of true football supporters, "Sneekes, Sneekes" was the predictable cry, plus a heartfelt rendition of "We are staying up … "

Five minutes later, Neil Clement's cross from the left wing met the onrushing BOB TAYLOR who knew exactly what to do with such a fine approach ball and buried his fifth Albion goal of the season. As he explained later: "We were really hungry against Charlton and there was only going to be one team who won it."

A neutral quickly recognised that, two goals in arrears, Athletic were no longer bothered. They were playing football like sleepwalkers. Sweating Albionites needed a little more persuading but when news spread bushfire-like that Walsall were now two goals behind, we knew. Oh we knew. The release of the tension which had piled up in recent weeks was both delicious and exquisite.

As the Albion players capered around the pitch, post-match, somehow it felt like a promotion but only because we'd collectively forgotten what a genuine promotion tasted like. Being football supporters, we could also convince each other over a beer or six in the sun drenched Vine and other local hostelries that this great escape was a turning point and better days were ahead. For once, we were right.

v Derby County 2-1

League Cup 2nd round, 1st Leg.
Att:12,183. 19 September 2000

Albion	Derby County	Referee
Jensen	Poom	Uriah Rennie (Sheffield)
Lyttle	Eranio*	
Clement	Higginbotham	
A.Chambers	Valakari	
J. Chambers*	Carbonari	
Butler	Bragstad	
Fox	Jackson	
Roberts	Johnson**	
van Blerk**	Burton	
McInnes	Kinkladze***	
Jordao	Christie.	
Subs: Sneekes*	Subs: Sturridge*	
Hughes**	Murray**	
	Schnoor***	

'**O**UT OF darkness cometh light.' Yes wrong club indeed but an apt description of the transformation that Gary Megson had performed on ailing West Bromwich Albion. His predecessor, the near comatose Brian Little, had offered only apathy and half-heartedness. In sharp contrast, maximum-effort Mancunian Megson knew exactly what he wanted and was not slow in making demands in very blunt language. Naturally, a relegation-bound team juggernaut wasn't easily turned around but the supporters were. A motivated, determined XI was considered a huge step forward by the weary die-hards. Any port in a storm was gratefully received.

A regular source of irritation was the club's dismal recent cup record. The Baggies froze far too often in knockout competitions; they were regularly and predictably defeated by smaller clubs. As for putting on a show against a Premier League side, forget it. WBA would curl up and die by three or four goals. The draw against Derby was perceived as just being our first chance to knock off a geographically easy new ground. It is Albion. Just turn up and do your best for the team but don't expect much in return.

A fraction under 3,000 Baggie people made the short trip. There were several dominant pre-match threads of conversation in the away end. These included the 20-minute safari from the overpriced car park along a dirty, muddy and puddled track; the teeming rain; the pathetic turn-out of Derby followers (who could only muster 9,000) and trying to make any sense of Megson's formation. Only after kick-off could we clarify the formation as being a strangling 3-6-1.

With Derby missing their key midfielders Burley and Powell, the theory was to cut off Derby's supply line. Danger man Kindladze was man-marked by Adam Chambers, a 19-year-old making his first start. The theory was fine except that the hapless Jason Roberts was up front on his own with no support either in the middle or from either wing. We were simply not going to score. But could Derby? Yes. On the 35 minute mark, DEON BURTON turned our Tony Butler all ends up and stroked the ball precisely into the net.

The Baggies wobbled badly, their confidence battered and lacking backing from a now silent away end who felt they'd already proofread that script too often. The Premier League side passed comfortably through our serried ranks. Fortunately there was no further score before the break. The horribly biased commentator on *Radio Derby* declared: "It's easy to get the ball back from a team like West Brom." Half-time was of significance to one prominent supporter, known to all as 'Sauce' as he had to leave for his night shift in a Birmingham factory. Oh dear. His mates told him he was the lucky one. Oh, they were so wrong.

Albion introduced Lee Hughes in place of the limited van Blerk. With the change of emphasis came a new attitude. Within minutes, Lee had already created and missed two opportunities. Then Derby's lumbering Carbonari made a right spaghetti of a challenge on the speedy Smeth-wick-born forward. The resulting cross led to a corner. From that set piece, the ball dropped kindly for NEIL CLEMENT who thumped the ball hard and low past Poom and the roar from the away end could be heard from our infamous car park.

The goal changed the game. Derby withered. The Baggies strutted and paraded their new-found confidence, urged on by the glory-starved 3,000 slavering with football lust. We'd never pulled off a good result at a Premier League ground before. Could this be our chance? The *Radio Derby* commentator became decidedly agitated: "This is a very poor performance from County and it looks as if West Brom could get the next goal unless Derby changes things around…"

Hughesie was regularly in full flight. Carbonari chopped him down again and then deliberately handled the ball. He was sent off for his second disciplinary offence. Seizing the opportunity, Megson subbed man-marking Adam Chambers for another attack-minded player in Richard Sneekes. Derby backpedalled even more, embarrassed and confused by the fluidity of their lower league opponents. Ruel Fox was spraying passes in all directions, Lee Hughes ran endlessly while Derek McInnes loudly directed operations from midfield.

Overall, the away support was already highly satisfied with the performance. A creditable draw on a Premier League ground combined with much mickey-taking of the home supporters was new and exciting territory. Yet the entertainment became better. Much better. SNEEKES received possession 35 yards from the Derby goal with only minutes remaining. Faintly, he could just hear the screams of his manager urging him to go to the corner flag to waste time. The Dutchman rarely listened to his manager and let fly. Seconds later the ball was past a static Poom and king Dick Sneekes was on a glory run…

Derby were shattered. Their few supporters were silent. *Radio Biased* was indignant: "A disgraceful performance from Derby…This man Hughes has turned the game on its head." It was our night and the after match celebrations were rich in exultation and simple joy. Of course it was only the first leg and a whipped up and full strength Derby would later win the second leg 4-2 to triumph on aggregate, but that night there was universal agreement that we'd all seen something special. The result gave us short-term reward and took the pride home from Pride Park. Far more than that, the victory offered so much hope for the future.

Never before had 1,000+ adults and children marched in single file through ill-lit mud, dense vegetation and deep puddles in such good humour. What does smelly brown ooze in shoes and trousers or the danger of falling into the neighbouring canal matter compared to a lusty rendition of "Gary Megson's muddy wet army!"?

v Bolton Wanderers 0-3
Play-Off Semi-Final, 2nd Leg.
Att: 23,515. 17 May 2001

Albion	Bolton Wanderers	Referee
Hoult	Clarke	R.G. Pearson (Peterlee)
Butler	Barness	
Gilchrist*	Bergsson	
Clement	Hendry*	
Lyttle	Charlton	
Fox	Frandsen	
Appleton	Hansen	
Sneekes**	Farrelly	
van Blerk***	Nolan**	
Hughes	Holdsworth***	
Roberts	Gardner	
Subs: Taylor*	Subs: Whitlow*	
Jordao**	Ricketts**	
Sigurdsson***	Marshall***	

BARELY 12 months previously, Albion had just desperately avoided the drop down to England's third tier. Now they were fighting for promotion to the Premier League. The nine months in between were often dream-like. The team regularly won matches; Megson instilled the side with a lunatic-level of workrate with special emphasis on brutally effective defending. Never mind the quality, just savour the results. After years of gruel and dry bread, this was a feast. Just extending the season with the play-offs felt significant, normally an end of season treat for other clubs.

The first leg in the Black Country was key. Amid a frantic atmosphere, Albion secured a two goal lead mainly as a result of flaky Bolton defending. Inextricably with a comfortable advantage within our grasp, unusually poor defending of our own handed the visitors two goals. The three quarters-silent Hawthorns knew the dream was in mortal danger. "We lost the plot," snapped Megson afterwards. Rumours at the time suggested that Bolton had big financial problems and for them it was promotion or literally bust. A long hard season was now reduced to 90 minutes in Lancashire.

The Reebok was quiet as kick-off approached, despite fireworks, a line of drummers and various other artificial 'environment-enhancers' – except for the double-decker away end. There a seething, roaring mass of blue and white humanity repeatedly boomed out "Gary Megson's Blue and White Army!"

But after just nine minutes, poor defending was again our undoing. BERGSSON stole in unmarked to steer home a floated Charlton free-kick ('steer home' being a euphemism for 'came off his knee'). Whatever the cause, to be behind overall so early in the match was wretched and Bolton were now ahead for the first time in the tie. But Wanderers had only won twice at home in 2001 so hope remained. The Baggies' following decreed they would remain in the ascendancy. The vocals boomed across the far from full ground. Unlike in the first leg, Bergsson and Hendry were on top of the Albion strikers; the Bolton defenders had a combined age of 70 and enjoyed a considerable height and weight advantage. This, combined with the whole defence playing deep to negate Hughes and Roberts getting behind them, was highly frustrating for the Albion team. Jason Roberts struck the outside of a post with Albion's best chance; Lee Hughes was a tireless (if often unproductive) workhorse across the whole of the front line. Kevin Nolan brought down Richard Sneekes in his own penalty box but frantic appeals for a penalty were waved away. The Dutchman was furious: "It was a definite penalty. I turned, he caught me on the shin but the ref didn't give it." There were increasing doubts that an Albion attack, heavily reliant on pace, could do anything with the long ball Plan B.

Still the vocal support continued even though there was precious little to get excited about other than reminding the silent, nervous, home Wanderers fans what a timid bunch they were.

As the game progressed, player fatigue increased and there was more goalmouth action at either end. The Baggies continued to look second best, and with 28 minutes remaining, Jamaican RICARDO GARDNER ran onto a fine through ball from Anthony Barness to score with his left foot. The away support sagged helplessly but then rallied once more. This was personal and we would not be bettered. If anything, the Albion support became louder and we even rose to our feet to give greater emphasis to our words.

Megson brought on all three substitutes and waved his team forward. It was a necessary though largely futile gesture. In the away end, there was only pride left and we had plenty of that. The stand flexed under the weight of 5,000 boinging Baggies. Prominent supporter Anc had every reason not to be at the Reebok but felt a compulsion. "I'm self-employed and had to work right through the previous night, getting home at 2pm. Yet I had to be there. I begged for tickets and ended up with the Bolton fans and very glad to be there. I will never forget that night. I think I was as proud to be a Baggie watching our supporters as I've ever been." RICKETTS applied the coup de gras with a third late goal. The dream had died – truth be told it was quite long dead – but we didn't want to admit it. Even Megson gave up. He admitted later: "I spent the last five minutes watching the supporters. It was more interesting than the pitch."

Only in the last couple of minutes were Wanderers supporters heard in any volume. It was thoroughly strange for fans going to the play-off final to be so outshouted by the losers – but were we really losers? The sense of community, of oneness took over. Despite the ending of the dream there were so many reasons to be proud to be a Baggie. The Dunkirk spirit had triumphed as defeat was turned into victory. There are some parallels with Liverpool in May 2009 but far more pronounced.

The post-match exchange of appreciation between shattered players and supporters was both warm and genuine – all too brief because apparently it wasn't our night and we had to give way to the Wanderers play-off final celebration which consisted mainly of more fireworks and an overwhelming PA system – just to drown out the away support? Everyone was hurting. Bob Taylor said: "I'm not ashamed to say that I sat in the middle of the pitch, crying me eyes out." Striking partner Jason Roberts could only manage: "I haven't a clue what went wrong."

We needed a collective lift after the match. Neighbours with misfortunes are always a rich source of top quality relief. As we journied home, Birmingham City and their tantrum-throwing manager Trevor Francis were going out of the play-offs. Francis's protests over choices of ends didn't help his players. Blues lost a penalty shoot-out and we all felt better. Albion had gone out too but with dignity.

v Bradford City 1-0

Att: 20,269

13 April 2002

Albion	Bradford City	Referee
Hoult	Combe	Mike Dean (Wirral)
Gilchrist	Jorgensen*	
Dichio*	Jacobs	
Clement	McCall**	
McInnes	Wetherall	
Johnson	Bower	
Balis	Juanjo	
Sigurdsson	Kearney	
Dobie	Ward	
Chambers**	Cadamarteri	
Moore.	Jess***	
Subs: Taylor*	Subs: Myers*	
Benjamin**	Locke**	
	Emanuel***	

NOT SO much the hare and the tortoise parable here, more a question of undesirable neighbours getting carried away and receiving their come-uppance. In early March, the Dingles of Wolverhampton were top of the pile. With only nine matches left and Albion ten points behind, frankly we were only considering the play-offs. As the Baggie faithful drove away from Selhurst Park on March 2, having secured a 1-0 win over Wimbledon, there was much grinding of Black Country teeth as a *Radio Five* correspondent reported that Dingle supporters were already celebrating promotion. But chickens were counted too early. The Baggies hit a purple patch of grinding out victories while conversely the Dingles could only find a crab instead of their bottle. Gradually, we wore down their lead via a series of increasingly sweaty, tense and (in the case of Bramall Lane) downright brutal encounters. Albion's resurrection was almost complete on Easter Saturday with Wolverhampton outclassed by Man City followed by yet another Albion win – 1-0 over Coventry at Highfield Road. Albion's determination, rabid support and the 'I'm not scoring today' Lee Hughes in the Coventry team were a compelling combination.

As the last curve of the Championship race became the finishing straight, the blue and white stripes elbowed aside the faltering old gold who'd lost again – this time to Millwall in a televised Friday night encounter. Having grabbed the pole position, we just (just!) needed to hold on to it. With three games to go, Albion's frustrating 1-1 home draw with Rotherham United, thanks to the referee being unable to spot Jordao's winner being clearly over the line, racked up the pressure even higher. (The draw also ultimately resulted in Crewe being relegated rather than the Millers – the call for new goal-line technology is nothing new.)

And so we travelled to Bradford to keep our dream alive. City were comfortably placed in mid-table, however this was the incomparable Stuart McCall's last home game before retirement and City had recently become highly adept at stopping the opposition from scoring. Hey, that's our game! With the Dingles turning out the following day, a win would give Albion a four point lead with just one and two games left respectively.

Partly to relieve their tension, many travelling supporters chose to dress up with a Big Dave wig or as a Black Country Hippie. The end result was colourful yet as a stress-reliever it wasn't helping. There were too many pale pinched faces. Once again, the fanzine sellers doubled up as stress counsellors. Even the seasoned supporter-drinkers who frequented the nearby Oakleigh pub looked far from mellow. Two Albion-supporting journalists chose to go for a balti beforehand but realised they simply couldn't eat it and were spotted shamefacedly clutching a large doggie bag in Midland Road. Other embarrassed looking Baggies were uncomfortably dressed in suits and ties. The away ticket allocation, although much larger than normal, was still far too small to meet demand and so over a hundred Albion supporters took the executive hospitality option at £100+ per head. Still more Black Country people choose to buy tickets in the home end rather than miss out altogether.

Bradford City were determined party poopers. Their unexpected resilience was aided by a nervous display from the hitherto unflappable Albion men and it was the home side who pressed the most. On the rare occasions that the Stars in Stripes advanced on the Bantams' goal, they found loanee keeper Combe in scintillating form. As a spectacle, the match made for wretched entertainment. For those who cared, it was a case of never mind the quality: a goal was first, last and everything. The team could not want for backing from the massed ranks of 6,000 supporters on two sides of the ground.

Following strong 'encouragement' from Gary Megson during the interval, the Baggies became more dominant but with little sign of a goal. We simply had to get more pressure on their goal even at the expense of our preferred they-shall-not-pass formation. Big Trevor Benjamin came on in the 65th minute as an extra forward followed ten minutes later by another – the incomparable Bob Taylor. The Baggies now had a wall of forwards and City were pushed backwards. Benjamin's diving header deserved to be the winner but the irritating Combe showed why he'd just been called up for the Scottish squad by diverting the ball to safety. Minutes later, Bob Taylor was left unmarked in the box but shockingly missed the target altogether. It was minutes that we didn't have – for as the game moved into injury time, there was still no score. Little electronic bleeps were audible all around as mobiles were switched off to avoid the torrent of incoming texts from jubilant Dingles. These were desperate moments.

City still hung on as every Albion man pressed forward. Bradford had a lucky escape when McCall gave Derek McInnes a hefty shove in the back in the box, an incident which the referee missed.

'In the 93rd minute' (a hitherto innocuous phrase which to this day now has an Albion meaning all of its own), Super Bobby Taylor cut into the penalty box close to the left- hand touchline and tumbled over Andy Myers's slightly raised knee.

A collective scream for a penalty went up and said spot-kick was given. There was wild cheering before there was a collective realisation of the implications. Our season rested on one kick of the ball. Albion had a shocking record with penalties with eight misses from the previous eleven awarded. There was too much time to contemplate possible outcomes. On top of Super Bob needing attention to his own knee, Bradford City extracted full value from every time wasting tactic in their book including painfully slow substitutions. Igor Balis was taking his first club penalty. Several Albion men had previously failed from the spot so the simple logic was why not let the full back have a go? Igor took penalties for his country but had only recently admitted that fact to his surprised team-mates. Was this the tensest single moment ever in Albion's history? Supporters were variously stood up, sat down, deliberately facing the other way, in tears, praying, clutching total strangers or all of the above. Some of the players couldn't look either. As Igor took his run up, my wife's head was buried deep into my jacket.

The outcome was simple and joyous. Combe was finally beaten as BALIS struck the ball into the top corner of the net. A sudden glorious farrago of joyously flailing arms, a roar of ear-splitting proportions and we're one nil to the good. Players, club physio Nick Worth and supporters rushed together in a mass touchline hugging session that the stewards were unable to resist. A universal stand shaking "Boing" was superseded by "The Lord's My Shepherd" and a heartfelt "Albion's Going Up" all infused with tingling emotion and belief. Rarely has life as an Albion supporter felt so satisfying. To keep our nose in front of the third place club was the bottom line but to do that by snatching it away from Dingle claws remains unique.

After a couple more sweaty minutes of wild kick-it-anywhere football, the points were ours. Albion had completed their 17th 1-0 success of the season. But we were not leaving that ground until we were pushed out and then continued to sing, shout, dance, honk horns and hug outside the stadium and across the whole of Bradford. Sometimes, just sometimes, football can be better than sex.

v Crystal Palace 2-0
Att: 27,761
21 April 2002

Albion	Crystal Palace	Referee
Hoult	Kolinko	Edward Wolstenholme
Gilchrist	Fleming	(Preston)
Moore	Granville	
Sigurdsson	Austin	
Balis	Popovic	
McInnes	Rihilahti*	
Johnson**	Mullins	
Chambers	Rodger**	
Clement	Morrison	
Taylor*	Akinbiyi***	
Dichio***	Hopkin	
Subs: Dobie*	Subs: Kirovsky*	
Jordao**	Rubins**	
Fox***	Black***	

OVER THREE hours before kick-off, the clans were gathering around the Hawthorns. Every local boozer was rammed as Dutch courage was eagerly sought. This was pure film script country – win the last match of the season to secure promotion to the Premier League. That was the elusive 'Big One' we'd dreamed about for more than a decade (we were young then and naïve). The top Division had somehow rubbed along without the Baggies' contribution for 16 years – the longest spell in the club's history. But the downside – and therefore the need for Dutch courage – was that any other result could mean the Dingles taking the spoils instead.

Around the ground, *Grorty Dick* sellers were under siege. Not just from would be fanzine purchasers but from supporters needing reassurance and counselling plus *Sky TV* camera teams who wanted yet another quote or visible emotion.

And there was much emotion to film. Young Bethany Lewis, attending one of her first ever games was alarmed to see her father Martin shedding tears prior to kick-off. His explanation – "It's because I'm here" – made little sense to his daughter but those like Martin who'd stuck with the club through all the dark times – Twerton Park, Woking, Saunders, Gould, Little – they knew.

Every side of the ground was a sea of blue and white and yellow and green. There were hundreds of flags too – many handwritten for the cameras including one glued (presumably with prawns) to the window of an executive box.

But oh bloody hell the early tension. Fingernails jammed into yielding palms, legs visibly shook. There were prayers to King Jeff for divine intervention. Most of the ground knew the Dingles were already ahead. We needed a goal. Get in front and we'd hold it. That was the law. Somehow it was right that 'Big Dave' DARREN MOORE, who'd been our inspiration all season, did the business, untidily poking home a ball which had ricocheted around the Palace penalty box. The noise levels were impossible to measure; tribal, primitive screaming on an enormous scale. Once we've collectively rallied, a massive "*Boing Boing*" was required followed by "*The Lord's My Shepherd*". It was emotional. "Are we in the Premier League yet?" asked young Bethany Lewis. It was a surprisingly fair question.

Albion had their one-goal lead and defended it in a manner which would have impressed Stoke. Our very big three at the back gave Houlty another chance to use his deckchair while the rest of the team hunted in packs. It would normally be enough. But one slip could still be fatal as Martin Lewis explained to his increasingly inquiring daughter. Sheffield Wednesday had equalised against the Dingles which provided some kind of insurance. When word spread at lightning speed of a second goal for Wednesday, the noise level was such that the players briefly looked very confused.

Then, early in the second half, Neil Clement hammered a free kick from outside the box. Palace keeper Kolinko could only parry and there, as we knew he would be, was SUPER BOBBY TAYLOR on hand to tap in the rebound. Bob ran to the touchline near the Brummie/East Stand corner where he and his team-mates' celebrations provided one of the most iconic images in Albion's history. Every supporter of that era has that goal and that celebration on automatic DVD replay in their memory.

A primeval roar to the skies. It was once more a sound beyond the capabilities of a decibel meter. The whole stadium was rocking, boinging, cheering and crying – probably all at the same time. There was still half an hour to play out. "We Are Going Up…We Are Going Up…" was bellowed with rare, convincing, urgency. "Are we in the Premier League yet?" shouted Bethany Lewis for the 12th time. "Soon…" was all her choking father could manage.

Palace knew their part and merely went through the motions. Albion's Scott Dobie should have added to the score but it didn't matter. Neither did Sheffield Wednesday missing a penalty against the Dingles and subsequently losing their lead. It was still like the Wanderers had lost it. "Are you watching Wanderers?" was a familiar cry in those last so laidback almost post-coital minutes and we had escaped upwards from the Nationwide League.

There was much pleasure in giving stick to Palace's Clinton Morrison. Bizarrely, he'd claimed beforehand he was going to score a hat-trick following a lost-the-plot public service announcement from the brown-trousered Wolves Chairman. Albion supporters hissed fury with Morrison's every touch of the ball. An urban myth sprung up that 'Big Dave' had had a few words in his shell-like ear suggesting that hospital food wasn't very pleasant. Morrison didn't muster three shots during the match let alone three goals.

The last rites from referee Wolstenholme was the signal for a mass invasion of the pitch. Barely a blade of grass could be seen yet all the stands still appeared full. There were scenes of such emotion, such fulfilment. Battle-scarred supporters were observed just screaming incoherently at each other as tears flowed freely. We gulped in the unfamiliar rituals of promotion – a lap of honour after 20 solid minutes of celebration and waving promotion banners. Camera crews were everywhere, zooming in on celebrities such as Frank Skinner in tears. Strangers were embracing inside and outside the stadium. The contingent of visiting supporters earned respect by applauding our players – and were themselves applauded for doing so. One Londoner boldly toured the running track, shaking hands with all and sundry like a member of the Royal Family. "It's one of my proudest days in football," said Gary Megson to umpteen reporters.

Meanwhile in the Brummie Road, a six-year-old girl heard her near-exploding father say: "Bethany, *now* we're in the Premier League…"

v West Ham United 4-3

Att: 30,359

8 November 2003

Albion	West Ham United	Referee
Hoult	James	Mike Dean (Wirral)
Robinson*	Repka	
Gilchrist	Quinn*	
Haas	Mullins	
Koumas	Daily	
Johnson	Pearce	
Gregan	Hutchison	
O'Connor**	Carrick	
Gaardsoe	Deane	
Hulse	Defoe	
Dobie***	Etherington	
Subs: Clement*	Sub: Lee*	
Sakiri**		
Hughes***		

THESE WERE frustrating times for Gary Megson's Albion. Relegation from the Premier League didn't come as a shock once the unwillingness to sign a goalscorer became clear. The defensive backs to the wall and pinch a goal performances of the Baggies in the Championship most definitely was disturbing. Albion were an expensively assembled side – where was the class, the style? Megson's very future was in doubt with informed sources suggesting that defeat at West Ham would mean the sack for the Mancunian.

From the outside, this appeared strange for a club sat in second place with ten wins in their first sixteen games. Outsiders were only vaguely aware of the friction between Chairman and manager with the former only too happy to find excuses to dump the latter. But the manager enjoyed the backing of many of "the great unwashed" as Jeremy Peace once described the Brummie Road regulars in an unguarded moment.

Some supporters were becoming rather restless. After the wrenching monotony of defeats in the Premier League, scuffed victories here and there in the second tier were insufficient to calm their pleas for entertaining football.

These were difficult times because other supporters were 100 per cent behind their previously promotion-winning manager. The two supporter factions rubbed along together with the subtlety of sandpaper.

Nevertheless, West Ham United in sixth place and with the best defence in the division were one of the more significant opponents. Over 2,400 Baggie people made the tediously long journey to the arse end of the capital, perhaps recalling the 1-0 victory there barely 12 months earlier when we dared to believe that remaining in the Premier League was not beyond our capabilities.

A few were still finding their seats when the Hammers found the net after just 48 seconds. A pedestrian Albion defence looked on as JERMAINE DEFOE raced down the right flank, ran at two retreating defenders and squeezed the ball past Hoult. When BRIAN DEANE added a second and then a third West Ham goal with only 18 minutes gone, the mood was ugly among the travelling faithful. "You might as well go home!" advised the home supporters cruelly. A few maddened WBA fans took the advice, rising from their seats and leaving. Bitterly tense arguments were breaking out between the pro and anti Megson brigades. Cross words, bile and possibly even punches were exchanged. Wet Spam skipped through the visitors' back line with such ease it seemed as though the Baggies players were wearing deep sea diving boots. West Ham were playing with bubbles but we were playing through troubles. When even supporters can't manage a unified front, times are grim.

With 25 minutes played, following a speculative long ball from Paul Robinson, ROB HULSE pounced on a mix-up between Dailly, Carrick and David James to pull one back with a toe-poke. Highly optimistically, a cry went up in the away end: "4-3, we're gonna win 4-3..." – a chant which was quickly picked up by most of the travelling Baggies. We always do gallows humour well. History proved that the last time Albion had recovered from being three goals behind in a League match to win was at Nottingham Forest in 1893.

Neither Albion player nor fan fully understood the significance of that first goal. According to West Ham supporters later, the first goal was the turning point, far more so than subsequent events. The home side had the jitters. Their passing was no longer slick. The dangerous Deane and Defoe were no longer seeing the ball. When HULSE spectacularly scored his second goal from 30 yards into the top corner ("my best ever," he admitted, though history later showed it was also almost his last ever for WBA), the mood had swung completely. West Bromwich Albion had real hope. All divisions were forgotten in the away end with grown men hugging complete strangers. "Come on, we're going to win this..."

Given the Hammers' shaky defence, another goal was possible. But what about our own back door? Defoe with the ball was virtually unstoppable. Thankfully, the striker scything into Sean Gregan in a shockingly late manner with both feet neatly solved that problem. Defoe's second booking (his first had been for diving) meant West Ham were down to ten men without any other fit forwards to bring on. No more attacking for them. Common wisdom among the chirpy away contingent was that the dismissal was not necessarily positive as the Baggies frequently failed to beat ten men.

Megson re-used a favourite motivational tactic. His team had only a brief rest before he led them back onto the pitch to focus on winning the second half. West Ham were playing their own games. The ground clock didn't restart for the second half and neither did the ball boys. Ditto their team?

Albion drove at the home side. The Irons simply panicked. After 15 minutes of total domination, the Hammers' debutant BRIAN DEANE, under tremendous pressure from Tommy Gaardsoe, completed his hat-trick from Koumas's corner... with an own goal! Cue mass Boinging in the away end. Now it was the home supporters who were spotted leaving early, serenaded by the travelling throng. The one way traffic was not over yet. They sensed it, we knew it.

Meanwhile on the touchline, Lee Hughes was warming up while telling all and sundry that he would score. Neil Clement recalled in footballspeak language: "I remember warming up with Lee, and he was getting a lot of stick from their fans. He just said to me he fancied himself to score if he came on." Megson grew weary of the ear ache and put Lee onto the pitch.

HUGHES kept his vow, pouncing on a dreadful punch from David James in the 78th minute. No-one who was there will ever forget that moment – that simple, deadly volleyed finish which meant so much. Lee ran towards the Albion contingent, hotly pursued by team-mates. Pandemonium ruled in the away end. A walking stick was spotted describing a high loop before crashing to earth, fortunately hitting only plastic. It was

Lee's last great moment in an Albion shirt. THAT incident was barely a fortnight away.

"Four three, WE SAID we'd win 4-3!" gleefully screamed Baggie supporters in unison. A flood of departing Londoners seemed keen to remind us that Rob Hulse had scored twice. Or more pertinently that David James had dropped two clangers.

There was still time for Hulse to complete his hat-trick but the linesman decided he was offside. And time too for David James to make a smart close-range stop from Paul Robinson. Later, a clear cut penalty was also denied to WBA but we weren't greedy, we just wanted the match over. The Hammers looked broken without any remaining offensive capability, yet watches were nervously checked and then shaken vigorously. And finally it really was all over... and the entire Albion team came over to the visitors' enclosure. This was no PR stunt, more a genuine outpouring of thanks to fans that the players knew had stayed behind the team and encouraged them even at 3-0 down (or so it appeared from a distance). A collective act of worship – raised, cupped hands, opening and closing like baby birds being fed in the nest. It was a classic 'I was there' moment.

For Megson, the extraordinary turnaround bought him renewed credibility and time to build a second Albion promotion side. West Ham was the key third game in an 11-match unbeaten run. Albion were top of the Championship pile and Peace had to keep his powder dry for another season.

v Ipswich Town 3-2

Att: 24,608

4 April 2004

Albion	Ipswich Town	Referee
Hoult*	Davis	David Laws
Gaardsoe	Wilnis	(Scunthorpe)
Moore	Richards	
Gregan	Miller	
Chambers	Elliott	
Johnson	Santos	
Kinsella***	Magilton	
Sakiri**	Wright	
Robinson	Bowditch*	
Horsfield	D.Bent	
Hughes.	Westlake**	
Subs: Murphy*	Subs: Kuqi*	
Koumas**	Reuser**	
Dyer***		

GARY MEGSON had a formula for winning second-tier matches. He stuck to it rigidly. The Mancunian's achievement in changing the whole direction of the club will never be forgotten. Yet it is the nature of football supporters that however many milestones are reached, they always want more. Many questioned the need for such negative tactics in 2003/04 from such a big fish in a comparatively small pool. The Baggies had a large, talented squad with parachute money to spend following relegation yet the rigid formula did not evolve. West Bromwich Albion were frankly boring their way to promotion, which sounded ungrateful after so many years of under-achievement but it was true. Home matches often featured a long period of numbing midfield boredom before Lloyd Dyer would come on to run at the flagging right-back and put in one killer cross to turn the game. Away fixtures were similar – scrapping out unnecessarily hard fought wins over often limited opposition. And yet, promotion seemed to be Albion's destiny. Whenever they lost a match, so did their rivals at the top.

With only eight matches remaining, WBA looked set for the Premier League. The previous four games all finished as victories as the Baggie Big

Blokes overpowered the opposition. Nine goals were scored – a veritable treat – with only two goals conceded. Promotion felt inevitable even though to date there were hardly any League memories to cherish from the previous eight months (the spectacular 4-3 at West Ham and the League Cup victories were honourable exceptions).

Ipswich Town promised to be different. The Tractor Boys had play-off ambitions as a minimum target and the Baggies had 21 years of hurt in Suffolk. This near Stoke-like bogey-team needed burying and we'd take any kind of victory to end that sordid sequence. We'd won 4-3 thanks to two late goals in September 1983 and had paid for that ever since with only two draws to show for eleven long trips. There was also the added friction of Georges Santos lining up for Town against Andy Johnson who had jointly formed a reluctant bloody centrepiece at the infamous Battle of Bramall Lane. Still if you had to go into battle, Johnno could take comfort from the close presence of the Horse, Greegs and Big Dave – all veritable mountains rather than men. (As it transpired, the two defensive midfielders studiously avoided any contact throughout the 90 minutes.)

Typically the play was cagey. To the fury of the demonic figure on the touchline, the West Bromwich Albion players dared to be quite sluggish and even more short of fluent attacking ideas than usual. Sakiri, the token attacking midfielder, was anonymous. To Megson's particular fury, the home side were occasionally finding some very dangerous positions. As early as the 4th minute, Russell Hoult reacted instantly to a point blank shot from Westlake with the defence waiting vainly for an offside flag. Even worse, the Albion keeper was struggling after both Santos and Gregan had collided with him. It was akin to being hit by a tag wrestling team. There was a question mark over the reliability of his deputy Joe Murphy under extremis so his continuation was highly desirable. For the rest of the first half, defenders took the goal kicks.

Disastrously, with only seconds remaining before the break, Town's MILLER eluded 'Big Dave' Moore to connect with Richards' cross. The goal was an unwelcome shock. So too was the blast of *Tom Hark* over the PA to encourage the notoriously quiet Portman Road mob to get involved. It was so artificial, so American in rural England and so unnecessary.

During the refreshment and red-hot-bollockings period, Megson made two changes. Joe Murphy had to take over from the stricken Hoult while Artim Sakiri lost his place to the sometimes exquisite Jason Koumas.

145

The Baggies weren't terribly good at chasing games as their set-up was designed not to concede goals in the first place. Urged on by the bristling figure on the touchline, they had a go. This was a Megson team after all and they would do what they were told if they valued their sanity. Jason Koumas's deft footwork gave Town problems, so too did the giant Sean Gregan who was getting his infamous large backside in where it wasn't wanted. Lee Hughes and Geoff Horsfield flogged themselves in all directions up front to make space for openings. Despite the endeavour, this match was bearing the hallmark of so many other previous Ipswich matches.

With barely 20 minutes to go, Albion won a free kick within striking range. JASON KOUMAS could be lethal at set plays. The Welsh international took his time and sure enough, beautifully curled the ball into the corner of the net via the post. He explained later: "I just felt that if I hit the target with my free kick there was a chance it would go in." His observation bore much of the wisdom of the Jasper Carrott line: "If it had gone in, it would have been a goal", but no matter. After a vigorous BOING, we collectively realised there was no *Tom Hark* accompaniment so improvised with our own acappella version. The natives scowled as if their mangelwurzels had contracted blight.

Within seconds, they had even more to scowl about. Their side were shellshocked after the Jason Koumas leveller and so didn't close down super substitute LLOYD DYER quickly enough. One gloriously powerful left foot shot within the penalty box later and Albion were ahead. Two Albion goals in two minutes? Quite extraordinary.

Cue an even more raucous home-made rendition of *Tom Hark*. The more the home supporters jeered, the louder we got. It's called 'terrace wit' guys – you should try it occasionally. To lead at Portman Road – wow this felt like an achievement worthy of a promotion side. Albion will comfortably hold on of course for a highly satisfactory win, as they always do from this position. Wrong!

Four minutes later, substitute keeper Joe Murphy was strongly challenged by large Ipswich striker Shefki Kuqi. Murphy couldn't hold on and BENT had an easy tap-in to equalise, despite Tommy Gaardsoe's despairing lunge. Albion supporters were furious, convinced to a man that Joe Murphy had been fouled. Gary Megson was apoplectic because he expected his goalkeepers to make the ball safe irrespective of personal risk, then argue about fouls. Meanwhile bloody *Tom Hark* was blasting out over the PA again. Sigh.

"A draw would be a decent result at this place," we muttered to each other, but with no real conviction. We'd fought back into a winning position, only to have it snatched away from us. The match moved into battered goalkeepers' recovery time. There were glum away faces in the away end – we were to be thwarted again. A flicker of interest as Jason Koumas brilliantly made space and set up Lee Hughes … Lee coolly found the Horse – was he offside? – No! HORSFIELD was all alone in front of goal … a simple sidefoot into the net. *Get in there!* Cue lungbusting choruses of *Tom Hark* and locals fighting for the exits. There is no way back when your side goes behind in the fourth minute of injury time.

This was a memorable 3-2 win. More than giving us an 11-point advantage over promotion rivals Sunderland, which they were never to make up, this was genuine entertainment and a long-time ghost put to rest. Since that warm April afternoon, Ipswich have become far more concerned about playing us than the other way round.

v Portsmouth 2-0
Att: 27,751
16 May 2005

Albion	Portsmouth	Referee
Kuszczak	Ashdown	Uriah Rennie (Sheffield)
Albrechtson	Primus	
Gaardsoe	Taylor	
Robinson	Hughes*	
Clement	Stefanovic	
Gera	De Zeeuw	
Wallwork	O'Neil	
Richardson	Cisse	
Greening*	Keene**	
Earnshaw**	Fuller	
Campbell.	Kamara***	
Subs: Horsfield*	Subs: Skopolitis*	
Kanu**	Mazague**	
	Rodic***	

THE ODDS of West Bromwich Albion being relegated were 1/20 according to the bookies. WBA were famously bottom at Christmas with only 10 points from 18 games and nobody ever recovers from that position, do they children? As usual, Premier League Albion had the problem of conceding too many goals while not scoring enough of their own. Two new arrivals to the squad in the New Year were to give the team additional impetus. Kevin Campbell, antique with zero speed but with Premier League nous and his own recording label, signed a contract. Meanwhile the cocky Kieran Richardson arrived on loan from Manchester United during the transfer window following some string pulling by Bryan Robson. The path was still rocky even for the cocky but by turning some likely defeats into unlikely draws (famously at Manchester City and Aston Villa), Albion hung on grimly to three equally moribund strugglers. In the last but one fixture at OId Trafford, the Baggies following couldn't believe their eyes or ears when the Stars in Stripes were awarded a dubious penalty. Spot-kick duly netted, they hung on against a none-too-bothered-if-Robbo-needs-a-favour Manchester United to earn another unexpected point. It was creditable, but the

Baggies hadn't won any of their previous six games so were hardly pulling up any trees.

The problem didn't lie with the opposition on the final Sunday of the season. Portsmouth had no more ambition than just turning up and dying on a football pitch to make sure their south-coast neighbours went down. The real problem was that Southampton, Norwich and Crystal Palace all had to lose or draw for WBA to retain their top flight status. Sky were overjoyed with their televisual feast but for the participants this was not to be a pleasant afternoon.

Portsmouth were perfectly obliging mid-table visitors. Their first choice forwards were conveniently not available with Dio Kamara and Ricardo Fuller vaguely filling their positions. The noisy Pompey supporters went out of their way to assure startled Albion supporters in Halfords Lane and behind the Smerrick that "We're only here to put the Scummers down". To emphasise the point, a number of away fans bought cut price Albion shirts from the club shop and wore them as solidarity symbols. The Police looked suitably confused. At least the Pompey crew had a laidback afternoon ahead.

Outside the ground, the atmosphere resembled a cross between a carnival and a ward full of maximally medicated psychiatric patients. The tension was such that even alcohol couldn't make any difference. One wrong word in the wrong ear and tears would flow. Yet inside the Hawthorns, ranks were closed and jaws set. If Albion were to fall short, it wouldn't be for want of backing – even from the away end. Bizarrely the south coast mob eloquently backed the Baggies, lustily joining in with our songs.

With nerves jangling like church bells, an early Albion goal would uplift everyone. Robert Earnshaw could have done just that. He was set up in fine style by Kieran Richardson but somehow missed the opportunity from 12 yards out. News reached us that Norwich City were losing – one down, two opponents to go. Southampton were briefly ahead, before courtesy of the exuberant visitors in the Smethwick End, we heard they were pegged back. But we had to win ourselves first. As former Albion trialist Ricardo Fuller broke free with only the Pole in Goal to beat, breathing simply stopped. But to everyone's great joy, he shot very wide. Was he fearful of his own supporters? Then word spread that Crystal Palace had fallen behind – but still no Albion goal even though Pompey were handing out plates in all directions. We were simply far too tentative, nerve wracked.

By half-time, Southampton were the safe club, which pleased nobody at the Hawthorns. Norwich City were effectively relegated, being three goals down while Palace were one goal behind. Urged on by both sets of supporters, Bryan Robson's men took a chance by pushing more players forward. It was a small risk; Pompey had all the menace of kittens. To bolster the attack further, Robson went to 4-3-3, swapping Geoff Horsfield for the limping Johnno Greening.

We heard Palace had equalised but an Albion goal now would make such a difference. Suddenly, marvellously, we had one. A cross from Gera handily deflected off a Portsmouth leg, and HORSFIELD calmly volleyed under the Pompey keeper Ashdown with his first touch. The ground erupted, including the away end. Within a minute, the away end supporters rose to their feet again, bellowing hoarsely. Southampton were now losing to Manchester United. Could this really be OUR day? Perhaps not... Charlton's Jonathan Fortune conceded a penalty and Crystal Palace's irritating Andy Johnson gave his side the lead with only 20 minutes remaining. They were now the safe club. A sullen, stunned silence replaced the previous buoyancy. Five minutes later KIERAN RICHARDSON wrapped the points up for the Baggies. Set up by a neat Horsfield backheel, Richardson's full bodied volley crashed just inside the left hand post. Rarely has such a brilliant goal been celebrated in such a flat manner... except for the Portsmouth fans, who Boinged furiously to set the example. Yet our game didn't really matter. Norwich were dead and buried, and Southampton also losing. Events at Charlton became the whole world. Rows of Baggies in the East Stand turned their back on the pitch to follow events on a TV screen in the executive boxes.

Suddenly a great roar swept around the Hawthorns... had Charlton equalised? Hatefully they hadn't – which only served to twist the emotional knife a little more. And then another even greater roar zoomed around the stadium... and this one was spot on. Jonathan Fortune had headed an equaliser against Palace, the side who used to deride Charlton as 'the squatters'. Well the squatters were enjoyably rubbing their former landlords' nose in relegation odour but their pleasure was nothing compared to the tearful emotion around all sides of the Hawthorns. "We Are Staying Up, We Are Staying Up!"

The match meandered gently to a finish. But what was happening at Charlton? There was an agonising hushed wait for the five minutes of injury time to be completed in London. Time took flight in a manner that surely proved the existence of the theory of relativity. More false alarms didn't help. Then, finally, the news and the almighty roar we'd all been waiting to hear – cue for half of the attendance to run onto the pitch, the South Coast gallery still wildly applauding as they joined in with a heart-felt rendition of *The Great Escape* closely followed by a lusty rendition of *Play Up Pompey*. It seemed only fair!

Many have strived for suitable words to sum up that stomach churning afternoon. Veteran supporter Martin Lewis suggested: "You're doing and expecting a 100 mph crash into a wall. Your life flashes in front of you, you think you're a goner – and then the wall suddenly disappears!"

Two iconic images still linger from that sweaty Sunday. As Palace's demise was confirmed, Geoff Horsfield and Albion journo John Simpson were filmed wildly hugging each other and punching the air. The other lasting image is Kieran Richardson sporting a Cheshire cat grin as he was chaired around the pitch. That evening, we really believed the Baggies were in the Premier League to stay. After all, the club had got away with mistakes over the season and couldn't possibly make them again – could they?

v Wolves 3-0

FAC4. Att: 28,107
28 January 2007

Albion	Wolves	Referee
Zuberbuhler	Murray	Uriah Rennie (Sheffield)
Robinson	Little	
Clement	McNamara	
Davies	Olofinjana*	
Greening	Breen	
Chaplow	Collins	
Kamara*	Potter	
Koren**	Henry	
Koumas	C.Davies**	
McShane	Ricketts***	
Phillips.	McIndoe	
Subs: Carter*	Subs: Johnson*	
Gera**	M.Davies**	
	Ward***	

SOMETIMES a match is won before the first ball is kicked. Horribly mindful that the visiting club were entitled to a big ticket allocation and no doubt under pressure from a nervous Police force, Wolves Chief Executive Jez Moxey made a decision that the entire South Bank, the spiritual home of Wolverhampton vocal support, would be given to...West Bromwich Albion supporters. The West Midlands Police saw the decision as a simple logistics issue – the coaches for away fans could be parked on the bypass – easy to guard and easy to access. The Wolverhampton faithful thought differently, emphasising the hallowed nature of their end and that those displaced would have to pay more for the 'privilege' (though their observations were expressed in more earthy terms). Moxey compounded his position as Public Enemy No.1 by offering displaced season ticket holders a free pie and a pint. This was his facile response to the vitriol heaped upon him and neatly underlined how little club administrators understand about the needs of football supporters and Dingles.

It was Albion manna from heaven. We could take nearly twice as many supporters as usual, have no concerns about the perils of the infamous Gobbing Gallery and ensure our 'calling cards' could be left all over the

South Bank. This unique offer tempted many Albion regulars who earlier resolved never to visit Molineux again after the violence in 1994. Best of all, we had a new song.

"Sold your seat for a pie and a pint…" had its first airing long before kick-off, rapidly followed by a reprise. It was repeated throughout the game until everybody in the entire ground could rattle off the ditty in their sleep. Just to emphasise our glee, an ironic "There's only one Jez Moxey!" also had regular airings. With the main Molineux choir ripped apart, the response was feeble at best.

Tony Mowbray, in charge for three months, was getting through to his charges (or most of them anyway), after a difficult opening spell. Gone was Bryan Robson's cautious, negative style replaced by a new emphasis on proper passing: Albion football. Attack-minded players such as Jason Koumas, Kevin Phillips, Joe Kamara and Zoltan Gera had far more licence to show off their talents. The defence weren't quite so impressive and in a worrying development, Russell Hoult was unfit, necessitating the introduction of notoriously wobbly stand-in goalkeeper Pascal Zuberbuhler. His position at the arse-end of an Albion player alphabet was more than just an accident of birth. His inclusion felt like being on a plane and remembering you'd left the front door unlocked. Were the Swiss international team truly that hard up for a goalkeeper?

With no parachute payments left, Wolves manager McCarthy was obliged to build a new young side. On paper, they were no match for Albion's seasoned pros. But local derbies aren't played on paper. The first half was frantic and combative but with little goalmouth action. Jason Koumas's driving run down the left touchline and measured shot just past the far post was matched by Olofinjana finding the space to score but Curtis Davies's leg fortunately intervened. Such was the backing from its new mass of tenants, the fixture felt more like a match at the Hawthorns with vocal volley after volley emanating from the South Bank while the old gold mob simmered. The imbalance was no help at all for a home side already struggling to make sense of their odd looking 4-5-1 formation spearheaded by the unknown and quite hapless Craig Davies.

From a Wolves corner, the ball dropped handily for a counter-attack when McNamara's shot was charged down. The fleet footed Kamara was away, playing a cute one-two with the astute Kev Phillips. Last defender Mark Little kept pace with the charging KAMARA before he ran full-tilt into his own goalkeeper, leaving the Albion man a simple tap-in! We'd have fallen about laughing had we not been so pre-occupied celebrating. Time for a huge BOING. We were still earnestly rocking the South Bank foundation as the players trotted off for half-time instructions.

Wolves made a double substitution to recover the deficit but the effort was in vain as within three minutes of the restart, the Baggies were further in front. Super KEVIN PHILLIPS was positioned in his classic edge of the penalty area position. He aimed to bend the ball into the far corner but onrushing Wolves defender Gary Breen got in the way, deflecting the ball past the highly exasperated Matt Murray. Cue for even louder celebrations. Another Boing. An impassioned *The Lord's My Shepherd* and another rendition of *Pie and Pint*. To either side of us, the glum Wolves hordes resembled bulldogs chewing wasps.

All the Albion team had contributed hugely to a fine collective and highly determined team effort. On that day, everybody wanted to play. Even Zuberbuhler commanded his box decisively. Now with a two goal cushion they could enjoy themselves. The impish Jason Koumas in particular revelled in the additional space and, oh dear what a shame, the Wolves side were looking very ragged. They looked even worse when from a Jason Koumas corner, ZOLTAN GERA timed his run perfectly to the far post to head home unchallenged. He celebrated with an impressive double somersault while we celebrated with a surge in the seats before bursting into all the old favourites plus some new ditties: "Can we play you every week?" and "We're just too good for you..." Hundreds of discarded free pies littered the touchlines, hurled there by disgruntled Dingles.

The one-sided score made for a laidback lazy Sunday afternoon finish. Not since 1978/79 had we so comprehensively put the Staffordshire team in their place. It was the stuff of dreams. Howling deprecations were levelled at the now departing fuming home support: "Go home, you might as well go home..." followed by ole'ing Albion's prolonged passing movements and even demanding a fourth goal. We could have had it too when Kevin Phillips set Joe Kamara up perfectly but the Senegalese blazed spectacularly over the bar when only six yards out. He was wildly cheered for missing. It was that sort of day.

Tiring of praising the Wolves Chief Executive, the new improved blue and white South Bank changed tack and bellowed "Moxey out..." but quickly finding that such a sentiment was being applauded by the remaining home fans, it was quickly back to our old favourites including "South Bank…" Even "Stevie Bull's a tatter…" had an airing. After all, it was too good a song not to be revived. Difficult to remember when visiting Molineux was ever quite this pleasurable. 90 minutes just wasn't long enough. Any chance of extra-time?

Just to make sure that our visit to the 'Custard Bowl' would not easily be forgotten, blue and white striped Tesco carrier bags were stretched over several hundreds of the South Bank seats. The display made for a picture to treasure in the *Express and Star* the following night.

But before that there were pints to sup and local radio to savour. "I'm not happy about it," lamented Mick McCarthy lugubriously. "We were beaten by a better side, a better squad, a stronger team. I'd have liked to compete better but there are no excuses. Sometimes you have to put your hand up and acknowledge you weren't as good as them."

There were an awful lot of Wolverhampton types to be dug up from wherever they were buried. January 28, 2007 was simply a wonderful day to support West Bromwich Albion.

46 v **Wolves** 3-2

Play Off Semi-Final First Leg.
Att: 27,750. 13 May 2007

Albion	Wolves	Referee
Kiely	Hennessey	Steve Tanner (Somerset)
McShane	Collins	
Sodje	McNamara*	
Perry	Olofinjana	
Robinson	Breen	
Koren*	Craddock	
Chaplow**	Kightley	
Koumas	Potter	
Phillips***	Keogh	
Kamara	Bothroyd**	
Subs: Gera*	McIndoe	
Carter**	Subs: Little*	
Ellington***	Ward**	

HAVING SUCCESSFULLY avoided our unpleasant local Stafford-shire rivals for several years before 2007, it was a shock to both Albion supporters and the West Midlands Police payroll that the sides would meet five times in one season. The Baggies were the better side in all three games to date (won one, drawn one and crazily lost one) yet were obliged to prove their superiority once more. On paper, West Bromwich Albion had a very strong squad (with 96 goals to their name) but in reality, Tony Mowbray was doing a Bismarck by holding the quarrelling factions together. Albion didn't really have a team, instead they had a collection of talented individuals who played as part of a unit when they felt like it and apparently got themselves sent off when they didn't. Even during such a vital period for togetherness, several of the team were already being indiscreet in their eagerness to jump ship.

At the time, the Albion media department successfully kept the lid on these selfish activities so the nervous 2,842 Albionites in the Gobbing Gallery were blissfully unaware. Although we were entitled to far more tickets than for a League match, the verbally battered Chief Executive Jez Moxey had words with the Police before trotting out the get out of jail phrase: 'safety issue'. Moxey was off the hook but we were back in the old routine, needing to remain vigilant because of the foreign bodies coming our way from above. Few other clubs feel the need to have away supporters sat below their own and all the others use netting to protect their guests from missiles.

Albion's forte lay in their attacking zeal, spearheaded by the horribly selfish but quick 'Joe' Kamara and the extraordinary talent of Kevin Phillips. Both had 20+ goals to their name. As Paul Robinson said of his team-mate: "Sometimes everything Kev touches turns to gold." Phillips had scored a hat-trick in the previous fixture – a delightfully relaxing 7-0 massacre of a young and disinterested Barnsley team. In addition, Jason Koumas was a remarkably talented individual playing within our midfield.

When up against such a powerful attacking force, the last thing the opposition needs is for their first choice keeper to be unfit. Rumours of Matt Murray's demise were not premature and rookie Hennessey was called up for his debut. It was a problem but the Dingles attempted to make light of it and even concealed the issue for as long as they could. They wheeled out some antique former Albion striker called Steve Bull to exhort their supporters to vocally back their team. Fancy needing to be told! Boosted by a maximum volume PA system, the mob noise was annoyingly impressive, providing the home side with initial momentum on a very damp pitch. It was so typically Dingles – effort and workrate but no class. Admittedly, however, Dean Kiely in the Albion goal was busy, making several stops.

But it was Albion who showed them how it should be done. Gary Breen's clumsy half clearance dropped at KEV PHILLIPS's feet. One touch…goal. Cue a prehistoric roar followed by "'oo put the ball in the Dingles' net? Super Kevin Phillips…"

Back came the Dingles once more, lurching forward in an ungainly manner, something akin to a footballing Addams Family. As half-time approached, WBA were looking relatively comfortable before conceding a soft equaliser as JODY CRADDOCK had ample time to head in Keogh's cross. It was Albion at their most maddening.

Yet, we knew our team could score again and Mogga's intelligent exhortations seemed to spur on his charges. They cut through or skipped over desperate Dingle defending. Paul Robinson agonisingly headed wide with the goal at his mercy; Joe Kamara's pace took him clear but he couldn't hit the target either.

And then… another grim moment. Wolves won a free kick. Set pieces were the Baggies' Achilles heel despite both the manager and his assistant being defenders. Once again they were undone. Dean Kiely blocked Bothroyd's free kick but couldn't hold it. The horribly oversized OLOFINJARA was quickest to react. 2-1. The mob celebrated.

We seethed, feeling as helpless and frustrated as Christians in the Colosseum. Was our promotion dream slipping away? Mercifully, our discomfort and doubt lasted only two minutes. From a Darren Carter corner, little KEVIN PHILLIPS was left unmarked at the far post and he produced another clinical finish. Cue one unholy din and a massive Boing. It was Super Kev's seventh goal in eight matches at the Custard Bowl. "Molineux has always been kind to me," he admitted later.

Meanwhile, after a lung busting 55 minutes, the home side did not have a lead to show for it. The equaliser rattled them badly and Albion took command. Zoltan Gera's addition to the team, replacing the industrious Robert Koren (or 'Frodo' as his team-mates called him), only added to the visitors' majestic passing movements. The lumbering elderly Wolves defence cracked under the strain. Taking advantage, JOE KAMARA made a trademark run behind the back four to run onto Paul Robinson's pass. None could catch him and this time he found the corner of the net to non-universal acclaim. It was to be his last Albion goal and his final 'my agent's on the phone' celebration.

Now it was the home support that was seething. They were goaded further by the classic *Pie and a Pint*, and *South Bank* chants (both references to the recent FA Cup match) and the evergreen delight: *Stevie Bull's a Tatter*.

Desperately, Wolves rallied in the closing minutes. After all, they were "supposed to be at home" as the Baggies faithful kept reminding them. Dean Kiely was again earning his money. Firstly, he beat out a powerful drive from Bothroyd, then during the tense minutes added on for stoppages, he brilliantly tipped Kightley's shot around the post. It was a heartstopping moment. Lugubrious Wolves manager McCarthy was to later single out Kiely as the difference between the two sides.

Losing the home leg is no way to make progress in the play-offs as we joyously pointed out to their fuming following when referee Steve Tanner blew his last. "Wemberley, Wemberley...we're the famous West Bromwich Albion and we're going to Wemberley..." Such moments and results ought to be bottled and made available on the NHS.

Despite much pre-match bravado by club and supporters alike, the Dingles knew they had little chance of success after their first leg defeat. In the return leg, the incomparable Bob Taylor exhorted the Hawthorns choirs (anything the Dingles can do, we can do better...) with remarkable aplomb, considering he'd never previously fulfilled the role. Remarkably it is rumoured he even coaxed vocals out of the Halfords Lane stand though that later turned out to be indigestion.

The Albion full backs went on to do a pragmatic and careful marking job on both Wolves wide men. With their main threat neutralised, it was only a matter of time before (inevitably) Kevin Phillips applied the coup de grace with the Baggies' 100th goal of the season and Albion were Wembley-bound. It felt mighty good at the time – little did we know then of the behind the scenes squabbling which proved to be a horrible drag on our final preparation. Rather shabbily, we were promised a lap of honour by our triumphant team which was later cancelled – presumably a crude trick to get the away supporters clear of the Hawthorns without confrontation.

One other unexpected outcome of the derby abundance was some mutual acceptance brought about by over-familiarity. It didn't last!

v Bristol Rovers 5-1

FA Cup Quarter-Final. Att: 12,011
9 March 2008

Albion	Bristol Rovers	Referee
Kiely	Philips	Mark Clattenburg
Barnett	Lescott	(County Durham)
Albrechtsen	Jacobson	
Robinson	Campbell	
Hodgkiss	Hinton	
Koren	Coles	
Morrison*	Pipe*	
Greening	Disley	
Brunt**	Williams**	
Miller	Lambert	
Bednar***	Lines***	
Subs: Kim*	Subs: Walker*	
Gera**	Igoe**	
Phillips***	Haldane***	

THE MODERN FA Cup encounter has a similar vocal support pattern to Premier League clashes – the team is compelled to set the pace and do something noteworthy to grab the attention and arouse interest in their followers.

Mogga's Baggies had certainly aroused interest after an initial apathetic 210-minute slog and penalty shoot-out against stubborn Charlton Athletic. Albion then flattened Peterborough's giant-killing ambitions with a 3-0 cruise on their own ground. In the Fifth Round, permanent patsies Coventry City were steam-rollered 5-0 with *élan*. Cheap admission prices persuaded 6,000 Albion supporters to pack the away end and their enthusiasm was infectious. How City supporters must dislike our regular slaughter of their innocents.

The smallest club remaining in the last eight were Bristol Rovers of League One. Naturally, all the remaining survivors fancied their chances against them. It was Albion's good fortune to be Pirate paired, albeit the plank walking would take place in Bristol. A place at the Big Arch for an FA Cup semi-final was 90 minutes away – the prize was so tantalisingly close that worries about indifferent League form would have to be suspended. But cynics pointed out that as long as the perennial dream spoilers Manchester United and Chelsea were involved, the rest of the survivors would only make up the numbers.

As kick-off time approached during the evening of a soggy Sabbath in Bristol, there was a new overpowering and heady mixture of tension and elation among the queuing visitors. Manchester United were freshly out of the competition, surprisingly beaten 1-0 by Pompey and Old Trafford. Astonishingly, Chelsea also no longer had any direct interest, having been knocked out by Barnsley. The FA Cup was taking on a whole new direction.

Joining the Tykes and Portsmouth in the Wembley semi-finals were Cardiff City. The best football team in the Championship could in theory deal with either City or the Yorkshire mob. So could the Baggies actually genuinely have a shout of *winning* the FA Cup on the 40th anniversary of their last triumph? Ominously, we'd been there before and blown our chance. With the field similarly wide open in 1984, Albion somehow managed to lose to Plymouth Argyle, two Divisions below them.

Rovers were a combative side with powerful forwards in Walker and 13-goal Lambert. They could boast recent visits to both the Millennium Stadium and Wembley and had only lost twice at home. Their club officials would do anything they could to help the Rovers return to Wembley. Albion supporters were agape as they witnessed an already wet and sanded pitch being saturated by hose pipes. This was a bad omen for those with long memories, who recalled a visit to Kenilworth Road in 1994. Luton decided that a paddy field constituted their best chance of victory and Town duly won 3-2 in a crucial relegation scrap.

The presence of cameras served to maximise the fear factor. Live TV wanted another upset and the piecemeal Memorial Ground felt like an appropriately down-at-heel place to find one. Half the away support sat in a golf stand covered with some kind of billowing tent material behind one goal. The rest found what shelter they could on a narrow strip of open terrace by the corner flag. *No Premier League facilities here, me dear.* Yet the Albion support was inspired not deterred by what the older generation might describe as a 'proper football ground'. With no realistic alternatives to entering the ground immediately, the away end rallied early, testing the foot-stamping capabilities of the planked wooden floor. The vocal battle was won well before kick-off. Rovers regulars supplemented by thousands of part-timers who probably didn't even know the words to their anthem *Goodnight Irene* couldn't compete with the stamping, raucous, hollering: "Tony Mowbray's blue and white army!" The unexpected rendition of the much-loved Liquidator over the PA produced an enormous roar from Black Country throats, hugely boosting noise levels. Even Rovers's exquisite pasties were insufficient distraction from the noise-making business for long.

Albion were at near full strength, featuring just one inexperienced reserve in the shape of local lad Jared Hodgkiss. The manager opted for physical power up front in the shape of Roman Bednar and Ishmael Miller. Top scorer Kevin Phillips was in reserve, resting his mature little legs, just in case his expertise was needed. As battle commenced, Ishmael Miller quickly caught the eye. The usually erratic striker was at his powerful determined best and Rovers defence were hanging on. To our joy (and surprise from what was a rare attack), JAMES MORRISON put Albion ahead, pouncing on a rebound in the 16th minute. The Baggies held firm against determined Rovers and when ISH MILLER blasted in a second goal of Regis-esque style on the half hour mark, our position just seemed too good to be true. Greening and Koren's silky skills were dominant in midfield but this is Albion, this was too good, and something had to go wrong. It did.

Rovers found the Baggies' Achilles heel of being unable to defend set-pieces. DANIEL COLES's goal from a corner made everyone of a striped persuasion anxious. Rovers were on top and they knew it. Albion looked anxious. Ish Miller was more like his normal self, missing a glorious chance to score. The interval brought relief and a chance to re-group. Albion were so close to their first semi-final for 26 years.

But in the second half the home side stormed at the Albion goal. One slip on a soggy and sandy surface would be horribly costly. Fortunately, it was a Rovers defender who boobed, diverting a routine long ball straight to the feet of MILLER. The big striker strode forward and scored with aplomb. Goodnight to you, Irene. Oh the relief and the joy. "Wemberley, Wemberley, we're the famous West Bromwich Albion and we're going to Wemberley". How many times can you bellow that and genuinely know it's true? These words needed savouring... and repeating again and again.

As if buying insurance twice over, Mogga sent on the incomparable Zoltan Gera and SUPER KEVIN PHILLIPS. Sure enough the old maestro found the net within minutes.

The admirable nature of a Mowbray team is that a lead is never big enough and they always go looking for more goals. With the third tier team in some disarray, ISH MILLER wanted a first ever hat-trick and got it with a precise cheeky pass into the corner of the net. Ish didn't normally bother with precision but it was that sort of night. Rovers had been torn asunder while Miller was enjoying what still remains even today as his best Albion display.

In one quarter of the Memorial Ground that will be forever Albion, the Boinging euphoric hordes, many wobbling precariously on their seats, raucously declared "We're going to win the Cup". With a 66 per cent chance of drawing lesser Championship opposition, we collectively dared to believe that night. Winning with such panache and five goals away from home deserved full reward. The five goals made a total of sixteen scored in the FA Cup that season. Such a goal-fest deserved reward. Anticipation is sometimes better than reality but right there and then it was so good to be a Baggie.

v Southampton 1-1
Att: 26,167
28 April 2008

Albion	Southampton	Referee
Kiely	R.Wright	Lee Mason (Bolton)
Hoefkens	J.Wright	
Clement	Surman	
Barnett	Perry	
Robinson	Lucketti	
Koren	Safri*	
Morrison*	Viafara	
Greening**	Euell	
Phillips	John**	
Miller***	Saganowski***	
Gera	Idiakez	
Subs: Brunt*	Subs: Dyer*	
Moore**	Wright-Phillips**	
Bednar***	Lallana***	

OCCASIONALLY, I have complete confidence in my team. I was convinced that we would score at Bradford City in 2002. Yes, the all-important goal didn't arrive until the 93rd minute and equally I could indeed have done without the penalty drama which preceded it, yet my inner belief was proved right. Earlier in the same 2007/08 season, I was in a minority of one at half-time who believed that Albion would equalise at Preston. Zoltan Gera duly levelled in spectacular style (though a later North End winner punctured my belief). So it was that prior to the tele-vised Monday night game against Southampton before an expectant full house, I was convinced Albion would find the net. In fairness, with over 100 goals to their credit and five goalscorers already in double figures, no-one before kick-off would disagree.

As a result of a sweaty but sweet 2-1 victory at Carrow Road in the previous fixture, WBA needed one point from two games to maintain their near biannual ascent to the Premier League. Yet few people are as adept at raising the stakes as football supporters. Now promotion was virtually sorted (the pre-match mood was that it was a done deal), the demand was to win the Championship. Not lifting a title since 1920 ought to be incentive enough but for the good of the game, the argument ran, nearest rivals bloody Stoke should not get their hands (and feet) anywhere near silverware. They'd only kick it up in the air or shove a cheese and bacon oatcake in it.

Opponents Southampton could not afford to turn up just to make up the numbers at a promotion party. They had to get a result themselves to have any chance of staying in the Division. A draw, worthy though it would normally be in the circumstances, meant their fate would be out of their hands so there was never any chance of a repeat of the infamous Germany v Austria World Cup 'match'.

Saints manager Nigel Pearson had inside knowledge of any weaknesses within the more long-serving members of the Albion squad, but even so, Saints' patched up penniless combo of youngsters and old fart loanees had only won two of their previous seventeen matches. Surely they couldn't keep out the rampant Baggies, the top scoring team in the Championship?

Unfortunately it seemed they could. Southampton had a belief born of desperation. Central defenders Chris Perry (another Albion old boy) and Chris Lucketti with a combined age that was pensionable used all those years of knowledge to be constantly in the right place at the right time. The home side quickly found the pressure of anticipated success quite overwhelming. Experienced star men, notably former Saint Kevin Phillips, were making basic errors through trying too hard. Very little coherent pressure was being exerted on the Southampton goal and Albion needed most of the first half to get their attacking moves together. And when they did, either keeper Richard Wright foiled them or a Saints boot on the goal-line would continue the frustration.

The dilemma for WBA was simply whether to stick or twist. A point would suffice so scoring themselves or launching an all-out attack offensive wasn't essential as long as the South Coast visitors didn't pull off the unexpected from one of their few raids. But the doubt remained a nagging one. For an under pressure and out-of-form side, the Saints were horribly quick and precise each time they broke, although thankfully their long range shooting was fairly horrible.

Albion's defence were notoriously wobbly under pressure throughout the season. The trick for the opposition, if they had the nerve and the firepower, was to attack the Baggies thus breaking up their momentum. As each minute passed by without any score, there were numerous nervous glances at the big scoreboards.

"It'll do," was the familiar argument. "Southampton will take the point and be grateful…" was another, along with: "It'll be a bloody nightmare if those buggers score."

But those buggers did score and for many it did feel horribly nightmarish. Saints teenager ADAM LALLANA ran onto Jermaine Wright's astute through ball on 78 minutes and beat Dean Kiely with the help of the far post. It was his first ever goal. The away following couldn't believe their fortune and celebrated with abandon. Were they going to avoid relegation? Elsewhere in the ground, there was wailing and blatant pessimism. Briefly the despondency was drowned out by a desperate roar of encouragement for the team but as the Albion cavalry charge continued to flounder against Southampton's massed defence, the mood darkened. Each missed chance – and there were an increasing number – was greeted with a chorus of ugly frustration and even a few tears. Even Tony Mowbray showed his desperation by bringing on the hitherto hapless Luke Moore who quickly added to the list of chances that should have been but weren't.

Yet I maintained my belief that Albion would score. Didn't we, according to the oft-repeated song, have the best midfield in the world? "Don't worry, we'll get it back," I opined confidently to supporters around me. There were many doubtful looks. But Albion were a team full of goalscorers. Someone would find a chink in the Saints armour. When Neil Clement missed a simple looking header from a corner, my belief was a little shaken but no more than that. Thus I continued to stand aside from the muttering tide of dismay. Watches and the scoreboard were checked again and again. It was horribly easy to imagine the Potteries hoof-men hurling their practice cannonballs with renewed excitement. Some Albion supporters actually left early.

They would be kicking themselves when CHRIS BRUNT restored everybody's faith in the capabilities of a fine Albion team. With only six minutes remaining, Viafara missed Roman Bednar's centre. Brunty made space with his first touch, and with his second he drove the ball between the keeper's legs leading to spectacular scenes of relief and of celebration. At the time, it was a joyously spontaneous moment (since then the thrill has been dulled rather by repeating the goal and its immediate aftermath at least twice every home match the following season).

In between fervent chants of the groundhog refrain: "We're Going Up, We're Going Up, We're Going, West Brom's Going Up!", the Baggies were urged to go for the win. And they tried... albeit briefly. Chasing the game under such pressure for what seemed like several hours had been draining and it quickly became clear there was no doubt the Albion side would stick rather than twist. Play slowed right down to a stroll as both sides settled for a share of the points.

The referee didn't choose his moment carefully enough to signal the end of the game and the teams were swamped by supporters invading the pitch. Some ten minutes elapsed before all the WBA team were able to escape. Paul Robinson was briefly spotted upside down but still enjoying himself before resurfacing, doing the breast stroke over a sea of heads.

Monday night is fine for half-interested television audiences but just so wrong for promotion celebrations in the flesh. By the time the pitch had finally been cleared and a relieved looking Albion team returned for their promotion lap of honour, the dull priorities of work or school the following morning seeped back into our minds. After all, winning promotion to the Premier League wasn't that much of a novelty for the Baggies. But at least the Championship was still there to win...

v QPR 2-0
Att:18,309
4 May 2008

Albion	QPR	Referee
Kiely	Camp	Paul Taylor (Enfield)
Hoefkens	Delaney	
Clement*	Mahon	
Barnett	Mancienne	
Robinson**	Blackstock	
Koren	Ainsworth	
Greening	Rowlands	
Brunt	Connolly	
Phillips	Ephraim*	
Gera***	Rehman	
Bednar	Balanta**	
Subs: Albrechtsen*	Subs: Rose*	
Moore**	Leighertwood**	
Kim***		

WITH THE final home match of the season against the Saints not quite having followed the perfect script, the Baggies needed to beat Queen's Park Rangers in London to ensure their first Championship since 1920. There was a fallback position with title rivals bloody Stoke likely to find a win-or-be-relegated Leicester City side anything but easy to overcome. Whatever happened, the visit to Loftus Road would definitely be our last in the Championship for a minimum of 12 months. Thus the mood for the vast crowd of familiar faces which gathered in and around the Springbok pub next to the ground on a warm day was relaxed and jolly. The season, with a fascinating diversion to an FA Cup semi-final, had been a marathon but one littered with numerous high points. Suddenly it was close to being all done and dusted. Many happy supporters took up the striking fancy dress theme of Superheroes – a fitting tribute to a Champions-elect side and for Super Kevin Phillips in particular. Even Laraine Astle sailed by in a suitably regal outfit.

Unfortunately Rangers have one of the smallest capacities in the Championship. Our 2,800 allocation, many with restricted views, was ridiculously small for the occasion. Security measures put in place by the

Londoners prevented all bar a few resourceful Baggies from witnessing the Last Day of the Prom(otion) from elsewhere in the ground. How to bring tickets and needy supporters together was a recurring topic of conversation on that balmy afternoon. How to get a nerve-settling drink was another. The interior of the Springbok resembled the siege of Mafeking. The nearby off licence was equally swamped by demand. For once, soft drink consumers had it all their own way with a separate non-queue.

Among the chattering groups of happy Baggies, there was universal agreement Albion had finally assembled a Premier League quality team playing in a Premier League style and "we'll be OK next season." But first – and this was the only buzzing insect in our smooth ointment – we wanted the Championship, mainly because we were universally acknowledged as the best football team in the Division but also partly to complete the set of promotion experiences. In the last decade and a half, Albion had earned promotion in second place twice, won and lost Wembley play-offs and been eliminated in a play-off semi-final.

The fixture was particularly poignant for recently returned defender Neil Clement, making his 300th appearance. His father Dave, a decent player with England caps to his name, had spent much of his career with Rangers. In a fit of depression, falsely believing his career was over following a broken leg, Dave Clement took his own life, exactly 25 years ago to the day. Clem is our senior professional and having endured some of Albion's recent darker days alongside the long-suffering faithful, deserved his third promotion.

Our celebratory mood continued inside the ground. When you've got Superman sat on one side and Batman on the other, it's hard not to smile. In addition to the regular paens of praise for our team, there were familiar uplifting refrains about promotion including bravado about what'd we do to Villa in the Premier League.

Curiously the Albion side seemed overawed by the occasion. The Rangers players presumably wanted to keep their places in their much trumpeted forthcoming nouveau riche era and were the more alert and 'up for it' of the two teams. The bovine-sounding Dexter Blackstock had a glorious early chance to give the home side the lead but fortunately didn't take it. The visitors looked tired, jaded, hot and nervous and were unable to impose their normal rich passing game. Albion supporters fretted and chewed their nails.

A harsh sending off was to turn the game. With eight minutes to go before the interval, Martin Rowlands of Rangers saw red for a high two footed tackle on skipper Greening. "The referee ruined the whole game," insisted the Rangers manager De Canio. Undoubtedly, the match turned on that moment. Dismissals against the Baggies that season were fairly commonplace (notably against Greening) and inevitably, they gave Albion more space in which to play their passing football.

The London side lost heart without Rowlands as if to say, 'we'd had our go but we've lost a man and its hopeless now.' Mowbray brought on Kim, switched to an attacking 4-3-3 and, urged on furiously by their multi-hued following, the Baggies started to play like Champions, switching the ball with bewildering speed and ease. The breakthrough came quickly in the unlikely shape of KIM calmly heading in Zoltan Gera's cross from close range. It was his first Albion goal. Deep down, we knew in that screaming, joyous 53rd minute that the title was all ours and Johnno Greening would be the first Albion Captain to lift a Championship since Jesse Pennington.

CHRIS BRUNT's spectacular free kick into the top left hand corner of the net sealed the win later but by then we were already convinced. "Champions... Champions!" was our refrain. Stoke were hanging on to a goalless draw as desperate Leicester battered away and the Dingles were about to miss out on the play-offs by one goal. What a glorious afternoon.

The remaining minutes were played out without further incident. It was curious to note that this completed the Baggies' 11th away win of the season, more than any other club in the Division. Quite surprising for a club regularly described as a soft touch on their travels.

Out came the presentation plinth and with it (gulp) a very large, impressive trophy. *Our trophy.* A moment we'd dreamt about for so many decades. So many players, managers, Chairmen and supporters had come and gone but at that moment there was an overwhelmingly compelling reason to be a Baggie. Adrian Chiles neatly summed up the mood: "I didn't realise how much it would mean to actually win it until I saw them lifting the trophy. It bought a tear to my eye, but luckily I was wearing a Batman mask." Not even the redoubtable Vic Stirrup, with his 84 years of support, had ever seen Albion win a Championship. It was notable how many curious opposition supporters stuck around to see the promotion party. In decades gone by, it was our role to be the faintly jealous onlooker. But no longer.

There were numerous moist eyes as the team and players gleefully celebrated together with our trophy. Had we known then that our football club did not consider this achievement worthy of a civic reception or had we been even vaguely aware of the oh-so-familiar Premier League season to follow, we would have stayed longer, far longer. Had we known we'd never see Gera or Phillips in an Albion shirt again…

At the time we assumed our in-ground festivities in front of a select few would be only the aperitif. A champagne-soggy Tony Mowbray pronounced: "This is a proud moment. When you think back to when we lost to Burnley on the opening day, we've come a long way and made a lot of progress."

As we wrestle with the Championship yet again in 2009/10, Mowbray seeking his own progress elsewhere and the trophy now sullied by Dingle hands, we do wonder what progress really is supposed to look like. But for followers of WBA, the imperative remains always to fully savour the high points as they happen. Positive results can be savoured at any level in any season. Trophies are special but there is always more to football life than silverware. Be proud to be a Baggie.

50 v **Middlesbrough** 5-0
Att: 22,725
19 September 2009

Albion	Middlesbrough	Referee
Carson	Coyne	Trevor Kettle (Berkshire)
Zuiverloon	McMahon	
Mattock*	Wheater	
Olsson	St Ledger	
Martis	Grounds	
Blunt**	A.Johnson	
Dorrans	Williams	
Mulumbu	Arca*	
Thomas	Yeates	
Bednar	Aliadiere**	
Moore***	Emnes***	
Subs: Barnett*	Subs: Digard*	
Koren**	Folan**	
Wood***	Lita***	

MIDDLESBROUGH – *what are they good for?* Up to recently, they summed up everything that was wrong with the Premier League – a League where largesse from a wealthy individual can maintain the status of a soulless, dull club in a soulless dull, recession-racked town, half-heartedly backed by a theatre audience – new supporters in a new ground, dumped in derelict docklands. Other than a brief flurry led by a former Albion man, Boro have never really overturned their Jack Charlton-inspired tag of being functional and boring.

Yet for over half a century, the Baggies were unable to win in the town. A few draws, yes – but mainly there was nothing else but freshly-coined curses for the Albion faithful to take away, as they beat a hasty retreat from the Smoggies' den. The bogey finally ended in September 2008, with a scuffed 1-0 win. The victory felt momentous at the time, and it was indeed the end of an era. Come the following May, Middlesbrough lost their Premier League status – and so did the closest thing football has to a length of twanged bungee-elastic, WBA.

New manager Roberto Di Matteo certainly made an instant impact on his Albion charges. By re-introducing the art of defending to the club, the

Baggies avoided their usual ponderous start to a Championship campaign. The Liverpool of the second tier (we hadn't finished outside the top four in our previous four Championship seasons, remember) were, this time, leading from the start.

By mid-September, Di Matteo's men were simultaneously top of the League and top goalscorers, despite regularly fielding a 4-5-1 formation, and regularly playing only in 'third gear'. A problem many managers would give their right arms for was that, if truth were known, WBA retained too many players who were too good for the second tier. And it showed. The Baggies were unbeaten after nine games which was their best start since the 1950s. Just behind them in second place were the Smog Monsters – whose squad of Premier League kids had coped surprisingly well with the rigours of the second tier, thus far. This was a mixed blessing for their supporters (had it really taken the shock of a relegation to make them rediscover the meaning of the word 'passion'?) who wanted a change of manager.

In normal circumstances, following the undefeated League leaders to the rest of the best would bring out the troops. But it was Middlesbrough – offering all the downside of a long road trip, with none of the plus points of Newcastle, Sunderland or Plymouth. Baggies Travel ran only five coaches (but eighteen were booked for a futile-looking midweek Cup match against the Arsenal Superkids, just three days later). Less than 1,200 Albion folk took their sit-anywhere seats in whatever Boro's anonymous ground is called these days – barely half that seen at the previous away games. Yet it's a strange paradox in football supporting that 'small is good'. Numbers may be drastically reduced, but with the 'us against the world' ethos keenly sharpened, and a greater feeling of genuine camaraderie with fellow fanatics thereby generated, a nondescript bunch of travelling followers can be quickly transformed into the legendary 'twelfth man', passion oozing from every pore.

Expectations weren't great because of the ointment flies already mentioned. Common consent decreed a draw would be a reasonable result, even though it would probably mean conceding top spot to the third relegated club – Newcastle United.

Di Matteo made a surprising team selection – 4-4-2 – with Luke Moore chosen to strut his stuff alongside Roman Bednar. The rest of the team was familiar; given the size of the squad, there were few alternatives.

Left-footed Chris Brunt was on the right once more. Albion's top scorer in the Premier League the previous season had been off colour in recent matches but he was to coruscate in dull chemical-land. Brunty doesn't half take a mean set piece. He duly lined up in the 17th minute, after Boro's Williams had fouled Moore. BRUNT's shot took a spectacular deflection off a defender, keeper Coyne was left stranded and the Baggies were ahead. Just taking the lead at Middlesbrough is a rare achievement, so a celebratory BOING was essential.

Barely ten minutes later, the former Boro trainee doubled the advantage – and traumatised Boro followers must still be experiencing flashbacks. Smoggie keeper Coyne was the guilty party, his awful clearance landing straight to Brunt while he was way, way off his line. Even so, being some 50 yards from goal, such opportunities are rarely taken successfully. Cue for CHRIS BRUNT to show his class with an exquisite instinctive half volley. "It could have gone anywhere," he modestly admitted later. Even an Albion great like Bobby Hope would have been proud of that one. Two goals ahead already – suddenly, the fixture was assuming dream-like qualities.

"You're getting sacked in the morning..." was aimed squarely at former Villa man Southgate in the Boro dugout. The home crowd also found their voice, an ugly booing sound but it was a reaction all of their own without club direction, so progress of a kind.

There was even better to follow. Not known for his heading ability, defensive midfielder MULUMBU's intelligently-nutted gem arced way above defensive height, and into the net. Heaven was suddenly Albion-shaped, and Di Matteo the deity that ruled it; justification enough to sing *The Lord's My Shepherd*, to lung-busting effect thereafter.

Moments later, the ref blew his whistle to signify the end of the first 45 minutes (or was it to spare Middlesbrough further punishment, a la professional boxing?). In the away end, supporters had a chance to partially descend from the awesome adrenalin-induced 'high' they found themselves in, not to mention phone the 'refuseniks' in their lives, to tell them, in unashamedly gloating terms, precisely what they were missing.

The second half was a delightful stroll. From front to back, Albion reigned supreme. This wasn't third gear football – this was turbocharged. Even two forced changes due to injury and the predictable trio of home substitutes made no difference to the classy Albion purr. The theatre audience moaned increasingly audibly as almost Mogga-like, Di Matteo's men went in search of more goals. And they came too albeit late in the game. ROMAN BEDNAR added Albion's fourth in the 82nd minute. This was an exquisitely-placed shot from the edge of the area, curling through a ruck of players. There was still time for the fast raiding JEROME THOMAS to add Albion's fifth goal. The wide midfielder motored past the despairing lunges of various home defenders, the ball seemed as if attached by an invisible elastic band to his boots, bouncing on his left foot, then his right before his cold, clinical despatch over the goal-line.

A 5-0 League victory on the road was a feat unequalled in club history for 32 years. What a remarkable pay-off for the Boinging 1,200 who serenaded their players with: "This is the best trip I've ever been on…" (shamelessly pinched from Hull City the previous season). Di Matteo expressed similar sentiments: "We have put a statement out for the rest of the League. We played well and we sustained it over the full 90 minutes."

Onward and upward, Albion (then probably downward again).

Bibliography

The main suppliers of source information were:

Grorty Dick Fanzine
Fingerpost fanzine
The Sports Argus
Sporting Mail
West Bromwich Chronicle/ Free Press
West Bromwich Free Press
Birmingham Post
Birmingham Evening Mail
The Express and Star
Birmingham Gazette
Various national newspapers.
West Brom's Cult Heroes

The private archives of Terry Wills, Norman Bartlam and Colin Mackenzie together with my growing note mountains also provided valuable inspiration, together with many uncredited individual newspaper cuttings.